FREE!

Ken Cooper

A Sequel to *Held Hostage*

"NOW THAT I'M FREE, WHAT WILL BECOME OF ME?"

© 2014 by Ken Cooper

Published by KCPM Publishing

P.O. Box 77160, Jacksonville, FL 32226

Printed in the United States of America

ISBN 978-0-692-21669-9 PAPERBACK

SCRIPTURE IS TAKEN FROM THE KING JAMES VERSION OF THE BIBLE.

MUSIC LYRICS ON PAGE 5 TAKEN FROM ROGER MILLER, "YOU CAN'T ROLLER SKATE IN A BUFFALO HERD," COPYRIGHT © 2002 STLYRICS.COM

MUSIC LYRICS ON PAGE 65 TAKEN FROM W.D. CORNELL AND W.G. COOPER, "WONDERFUL PEACE."

MUSIC LYRICS ON PAGE 135 TAKEN FROM ALBERT BRUMLEY, "I'LL FLY AWAY!"

"IF I'M GONNA BE FREE, I'VE GOTTA BE ME!"

Foreword

In the last scene of *Held Hostage,* after Ken's release from prison, the author zoomed along with me, his wife-to-be, on a north Florida beach in my black MGB convertible. He stood up and bellowed, "I'm free! I'm free! I'm free!"

I let go of the steering wheel, raised my hands, looked up at him and shouted, "And, you're forgiven!"

But in the sequel, the second of a three-part autobiography, the former "Gentleman Bank Robber" who took hostages at some of the banks, finds that countless people had not forgiven him. He also discovered that freedom to pursue the American Dream outside prison was hard to grasp and even harder to hold on to.

As he attempts to adjust to "street life" by finding a job, he learns that the right to work is defined not only by employers' perspective of him, but by the criminal label he would carry throughout life, although he obviously could not serve out the 99-year life sentence imposed by the court for a 13-year crime spree.

When the Florida Parole Commission paroled him, dismayed law enforcement officials and the sentencing judge vehemently opposed his release. The basis of their opposition could be summed up as follows:

A serial criminal controlled and driven by a dangerous adrenaline addiction cannot be trusted to function as a law abiding citizen since he did not receive effectual addictions recovery treatment in prison for his long term out-of-control behavior that demanded his removal from society to protect the public.

● ● ●

i

FREE
By Ken Cooper

Hard core criminals afflicted with addictions that keep them behind bars expressed their opinion in convict vernacular that gnaws of sarcasm: "The Big Dog in Ken Cooper hasn't been tamed, and he will prowl again!"

In *Free!* Ken admits that at freedom's gate he struggled with fear that he would reoffend. The root causes of the addiction had not been dealt with.

The narrative is written in first-person, and my favorite chapters are the early ones that tell about our relationship and involve the reader in our engagement, marriage and honeymoon. *Very romantic, real with lots of joy, awakenings and fun. Enjoy!*

Then midway through this second part of his biography my husband shares a gripping turning point experience that confirmed his redemption and brought back a sense of dignity and destiny: a foot-washing that humbled and cleansed him while doing the same for the convict-hater who washed his feet.

At this point Ken says he realizes that freedom is a double-edged sword that cuts two ways and divides society between people who label and reject him without knowing him, and those who receive him freely with an unabashed, unconditional forgiveness.

Of the latter people Ken says, "Their amazing unconditional love cut me loose from my shameful past, and the shackles of guilt fell away to reveal the free man I could be in Christ. In these flashes of a new reality, the *Big Dog's* growl became a whimper as a powerful new person, who could control the *Big Dog*, began to emerge from within.

• • •

"Also, I saw the hand of *God, the Potter,* continue to break and remold me. Somehow, this painful therapeutic experience empowered me to believe that each day's doing, not yesterday's dark deeds, would define my destiny rather than the criminal stigma many people branded me with."

I shared his vision, but I also saw him continue to grapple with the truth that God's ransom from addiction was real for him only when he died to his despised negative self image, the addict/thief, *the Big Dog,* as he calls it, that drove the *getaway car* during his thirteen-year crime jaunt. He says this was virtually impossible since it required him to forgive public-enemy-number-one, himself, for the suffering he inflicted on victims including bankers, bank tellers, family, friends and people he had never met.

I hope you enjoy and benefit from reading *Free!* as much as I did from living and growing with Ken as he learned how to cope with the possibilities and responsibilities of freedom that define his destiny.

Proudly, in Christ,

June Cooper

* * *

Dedication

To my beloved wife, mother and daughter...
To family and those who welcomed me "home"
and walked with me on my freedom journey

To the bank tellers and all the other victims held
hostage by my depravity. I continue to
pray for their healing and forgiveness

To all the repentant criminals behind prison bars
waiting their turn at freedom's gate

Laughing Gull Laughs Last
About the Book Covers

"The Laughing Gull lives up to its name calling a loud and raucous *ha-ha-haa-haa-haaa*. They are aggressive feeders, using free-wheeling flight skills to snatch fish from pelicans' pouches and steal food from other birds. This and their mask-like black head earn them the nickname, 'bandits of the sky.'" [Many convicts in Florida's coastal prisons identify with them and dream of being as free as they are.]

George Register
Weekly prayer partner of Ken Cooper

In Tribute

The late HOWARD CONNELL, known as Maurice and Moe in *Held Hostage* and *Free!* stood by me and with me during two brutal years at *the Rock* and through the agonizing last two weeks of lockup at Lawtey Correctional. I hope you can read this tribute in heaven, Moe.

The late DAN JONES: Dan Jones ERA Realty and Christian Civic leader. With raucous, uproarious laughter and fun he dragged me to countless speaking engagements and meetings God used to restore a sense of personal worth and belonging. *Free!* is an accolade to you, Dan.

HUGH JONES, former President of the Barnett Bank, Jacksonville, reached out to me in love upon my release. A victim of bank robberies, he encouraged me to love myself, and still does in every imaginable way.

The late BOB MURRAY, a Missouri ex-offender turned minister, a great friend, who kept after me to "journal" the anecdotes, issues and thoughts that would become key elements of the manuscript. And I thank you, Bob, for showing me how to step out in faith to find God's purpose for my life.

The late JAMES WHYTE served as my work release sponsor and mentor, not an easy task for him or me, until I was ready to leave his employment at The Florida Times-Union for ministry. The final chapters are dedicated to you, my hero, who wrote me weekly during the last year in prison to help prepare me for release and reintegration.

Special Thanks

June for living with me and helping me through those early years of my search for freedom. I am deeply grateful to our children, Becky, Bruce, their six children who have given us thirteen great grandchildren.

Restoration Baptist Church, Rev. Doyle Harper, pastor, and my immediate church family in Jacksonville.

Bob Edmunds, Dugger Jamison, Ray Murray, the late Ron Oglesby, and Jack Smith, who encouraged me to write *Held Hostage* and *Free!* while supporting the prison ministry that kept the projects alive.

Paul Pinkham, award winning journalist and author, who provided final proofreading and editing.

All those who helped with editorial feedback in the telling of the story: Dr. Jimmy Crosby, Michael McPhillips, Donna and Earl Porter, Frank and Judy Pelot, George Register, Julie and Mike Seals, Bill and Linda Tasseff, John Pelot, manuscript formatting and computer art work..

KCPM Board of Directors: Rev. Doyle Harper, Rev. Ernest Setzler, Dugger Jamison, George Register, Bill Tasseff, Linda Tasseff, Jeff Harper, Michael McPhillips, Jo An McPhillips, Roger Jones, Larry Ries. (Ron Oglesby, Nick Perrone, deceased.) Without your prayers, financial support and guidance there would be no book.

KCPM grad, Gary Bell, did the art work for the cover.

To the 2500+ graduates of Ken Cooper Ministries transition residency services, who thrive as law-abiding, tax-paying, contributing citizens through our Lord, Jesus Christ. The annual economy impact of their transformation for Florida is a whopping $75 million.

* * *

Acknowledgments

Listed in chronological order, the people God used to stop my crime spree and those He used to set me free from state prison in less than four years on 99:

The UNNAMED POLICE OFFICER, who stopped the 13-year-crime-spree with one shot and said in a recent email that he was thankful he was a Christian at the time, or he would have pulled the trigger twice. I responded, "You think you're thankful. I'm really thankful; I would probably be in Hell today!"

The late SYD BARRETT, retired school teacher, minister for ABE BROWN PRISON MINISTRY, visited me in a Tampa jail and led me to accept the Lord, Jesus Christ, as my Savior before I was sentenced to serve 99 years.

The late HONORABLE JUDGE HARRY L. COE, Tampa, sentenced me to 99 years and retained his jurisdiction over me for 33 years. DOC branded me as dangerous and classified me as a "lifer" who would die in prison at *the Rock* at Raiford, Fla. It turned out God had other plans. Judge Susan Black closed *the Rock*, the first step toward freedom's gate at Lawtey Correctional.

KY KOCH, a Christian attorney of Clearwater, Fla., worked miracles through which kidnapping and other charges were dropped, and without fee, obtained the sentencing judge's release of his 33 years jurisdiction!

FLORIDA DEPARTMENT of CORRECTONS provided the security and programs I needed. CHAPLAINS ELDON CORNETT, the late LARRY SHOOK of Union Correctional;

* * *

ROY MORRISON and BARRY MYERS, volunteer chaplain, of Baker CI and JOHN STRICKLAND, Lawtey CI, helped me achieve freedom in prison.

NEAL STAVELY, prison classification officer at Baker CI, recommended parole three years into my sentence. God used this fantastic miracle to set me free!

The FLORIDA PAROLE COMMISSION granted parole despite a judicial objection, and seven parole officers provided the tough but fair parole conditions I needed to find my place in a "free" world.

RAYMOND DUNCAN, Time for Christ Ministry, sacrificed his time and risked his reputation to achieve my early release and parole!

BOBBY MARTIN, Vice President and Director of Operations, The Florida Times-Union, supported and encouraged me from my first day of freedom until now.

The KAIROS PRISON MINISTRY FAMILY: "Through the unconditional love of Christ you taught me that freedom is living in God's Spiritual Time, not the absence of prison bars."

Author's Note

I did my best to accurately describe every incident and anecdote as they happened those many years ago. Due to the time lapse since the dialogues occurred, the conversations are paraphrased at best, but I took great care to express the essence and spirit of the verbal exchanges. Please note that I *italicized* the thoughts and conversations with myself in order to invite the reader into my mind where he or she is more apt to experience my emotions.

1

My last evening in prison at Lawtey Correctional, a transition facility located some forty miles southwest of Jacksonville, Florida, was spent with my best friends and other inmates who stopped by the bunk to bid me goodbye.

I expected Christian brothers I had done hard time with at *the Rock* at Raiford to be among the first from the seventy-two man dorm. But I was in no way disappointed when it turned out to be a young inmate I'd known for only two weeks during my short stay at Lawtey, as I was headed to work release in Jacksonville, my final freedom gate.

The first inmate was a child-man whose given name was Nathan, but his Bible toting buddies called him Nathaniel: "a man of God without guile."

In my few contacts with him I observed that he possessed the integrity, faith and spiritual curiosity of a big-eyed child and looked the part. In appearance, the antithesis of a hard core criminal, he stood about five-foot-five, sported a mop of blond hair over bright blue eyes. He seemed to love everyone, even the evil convicts who persecuted him sorely for his perceived physical weakness and for his devotion to God. He apologized for approaching the foot of my cot: "Sorry to uh, to barge in on your last evening, but uh, before you go, uh, uh, last night... I have a scripture the Lord gave me for you."

"Thanks, brother, I could use an uplifting word right now...for some reason I'm scared I won't make it out the gate," I replied without a smile.

"Uh, uh, you're dead serious...you're afraid one of the crazy thugs..uh, my evil "pals" will jam your time?" he said with a question mark in his voice.

"Not really, but I'm real antsy, probably won't sleep a wink tonight, worried the law won't let me walk through the gate."

"Relax, Mr. Cooper, you'll make it out alright; that's what this scripture is about," he said as he showed me a Bible in his hand.

His message of hope made me eager to read the scripture "Gimme, gimme," I begged, laughing, as he opened the Bible to a passage in the Old Testament, near the beginning of the well worn book.

"Here it is, brother," he said as he turned to a page where a black ribbon served as a bookmark, handed the Bible to me and stammered, "You...uh, you must read a lot better than me...I marked the verse and put your name by it...r...re..read it all."

I took the Bible in hand, located the underlined passage, *1 Samuel 2:8*, and read it out loud from the old King James English version favored by most convicts, but omitted the *eths*: "He raises up the poor out of the dust, and lifts the beggar out of the dunghill, to set them among princes, and to make them inherit the throne of glory for the pillars of the earth are the Lord's..." Beyond the word, *Lord's*, I didn't feel like reading as the wonder in my heart rushed into my face and filled my eyes with tears. Two weeks earlier when I approached the gate at Baker CI, to be transferred to

2

Lawtey, an inmate named Ernest came to me with the very same prophetic message, but from a different passage of scripture, Psalm113:7-8. *This blows my mind but I can't receive it right now*, I thought as I felt my face grow hotter with a second rush of blood.

"It's you, Brother; it's a prophecy for you...You will sit among princes!" Nathaniel shouted loud enough with his high pitched voice that the officer making his rounds jerked a look at him, but went on about his business at the laid back facility.

Faces of "princes" I once sat with: Prince Philip and Princess Anne of England, governors, celebrities flashed before me and I remembered how far I'd fallen, how much it hurt to be counted among the state's most dangerous criminals at *the Rock*, and how impossible I felt it would be to ever sit among princes again. My mind couldn't receive Nathaniel's message, so I said, "That blows me away, pal! I want to go back to that highlife, but it feels so far away."

"I didn't have many good things to remember so it may not be as hard for me," he said.

"The way you've turned out; seems to me you have great parents and memories, pal."

"A couple of foster parents, never knew my real mom and dad, but every day now with Jesus, I'm making good memories for out there?"

"What a good attitude, but for me, tonight, the flashes of the really great times make me think I'll never make it back."

"You will, 'cause this promise is from God's word."

"Coming from you, Nathaniel, I should be able to receive it, but honestly, right now I can't worry about anything but walking through the gate tomorrow morning."

"Oh, uh, I understand, but uh, some day...uh, you'll remember...what God told you," he said.

I got up, hugged Nathaniel like he was my son and said, "If I never hug another one, I'm hugging a prince right now."

My young friend returned my embrace, blushed and whispered, "See you later, Brother Cooper, but not here."

I laughed, but out of the corner of my eye, I saw a figure in blue rushing toward me. A supercharge of adrenaline shot into my blood stream, and I turned to defend myself against a deranged convict like I'd done at *the Rock*. But when I focused on the intruder, I chortled like a mad man and to myself, I said, *It's Moe, definitely crazy but not a thug. Thank God!*

With his guitar in one hand and a Batman comic book in the other, my little buddy skipped happily down the aisle on my side of the steamy dormitory. I thanked God again, this time that an officer had not seen Maurice breaking the "no running" rule. "Wonder if that includes skipping?" I mused out loud.

True to his wound-up troubadour nature, he announced his arrival by throwing the comic book on the bunk and shaking his shag of brown hair for affect. He sat erect on the foot of the cot, held my eyes with his as if he were a performer on stage and celebrated my home going with a song he had written for the occasion.

Maurice the musician plucked the strings of his old guitar. He was an accomplished picker and singer and possessed a great sense of humor. With Roger Miller, the popular country singer, he had written songs like *Dang Me, Take a Rope and Hang Me,* and *You Can't Roller Skate in a Buffalo Herd.* But, from the very first word of this new number, I heard the wrong song: *"The poleece and the judges, the bankers and people in the church pew will welcome you..."*

He stopped in mid-sentence. The sound coming out of his guitar didn't match the true pitch of his soft tenor voice. The instrument's strings were old and stretched beyond retuning, but true to his never-say-die nature, Moe would try and try... and try me as he attempted to tune the strings.

I grinned through gritted teeth and thanked God he had stopped singing. Clever sarcastic lyrics about police, judges and bankers welcoming me stirred up skyrocketing emotions. As my mind raced toward the prison exit I clung tight to an emotional rollercoaster that plunged from ecstatic highs to morbid lows as it careened around my mind's fast track to Jacksonville.

As Moe attempted to tune his guitar, fear in my gut rose up and made a threatening accusation: *Less than four years in prison on ninety-nine is absurd. One call from one victim: they'll come for me at the gate, and justice will be served.*

While he continued to fiddle with his guitar, I tried to imagine myself skipping like Moe through the iron-barred exit but I couldn't. *An armed robber who victimized hostages and held up banks for thirteen years...There's no way they'll let me go...This is too good to be true.*

FREE
By Ken Cooper

As Moe plucked some more, I stalked to and fro pursuing answers to several questions: *Am I still hooked on the adrenaline juice that drove me from one bank to the next? Even while I was director of advertising for the state of Kentucky...even though I made more money than the governor...I couldn't resist the crazy urge to holdup a bank now and then...Have I actually changed? The fact that I repented of my sins and asked Christ into my life... will that be enough? Is it just jailhouse religion? Oh, God, help me! I may not be ready... why can't Moe sing a freedom ballad,, one that gives me hope I'll make it outside ... whether I deserve to be free or not?*

Moe glanced my way and stopped tuning his instrument. His bright brown eyes beneath shaggy dark eyebrows pierced mine. He thumped his chest and proclaimed, "Mr. Pace Maker, give me just a few beats of your last eleven hours."

I looked at him coldly and didn't respond.

An avid Batman fan, he continued, "Where's your heart? You pace like the Penguin and flinch like the Joker since you heard the first words of the first verse."

"I doubt it, *Robin*; a ballad beginning with the words *police, judges* and *bankers is about* my crazy life of crime."

"What's up with that, Ninety-nine?" he asked, calling me by the old brutal *Rock* nickname. "You look like a wounded warrior suffering from PITS." A well read, bespectacled man who could have passed for a college professor, Maurice used an acronym he coined for the suffering ex-prisoners go through after their release: Post Institution Trauma Syndrome.

6

"Yeah like wounds from *the Rock*...but what gives? You haven't called me 'Ninety-nine' since our bloody days in that hell hole?"

"You'd better adjust your mask, Coop. Like a wounded warrior headed home from war; you'll flash back to prison scars at the gate."

"Your song is not about that, Moe?"

"No, it's about the freedom road ahead. It's about the ransom notes posted along the way..."

To stop the silly tirade I gripped his arm and declared, "The beginning sure didn't sound like..."

Moe withdrew his arm and interrupted me, "Okay, okay, it's a ballad about a notorious gentleman bank robber going home early, '*Three on Ninety-nine.*'"

He guffawed and for a moment, I joined him, but after a few gasps for air, the laughter stuck in my throat and became a sour tasting paranoia. I had relived the last bank robbery and "my bloody fall" a thousand times: the horror on the face of the teller who stuffed the bag full of money, the adrenaline rush that made me feel like Superman, the ominous terror-filled eyes of the officer as he raised his gun to shoot me, the slug speeding toward me in slow motion, the fire in my chest, darkness and waking up in my spilt blood.

"Moe, you may cause me to die of PITS!"

"No, I won't and you're going to be okay, too."

"What makes you say that?"

The look on Moe's face showed he loved the moment. He stood up, assumed a professorial stance and gave me a short lecture: "To escape the reality of being locked away

7

from the outside world and separated from loved ones, a
prisoner doomed to die in chains of old age... spends his
hours inside his head, in a land of fantasy."

"I get the picture, pal, I lived it: at night, I flew all
over the place."

"You couldn't' escape bodily; you did it mentally."

"Yeah, in fantastic dreams, I flew back to the past, to
good times in the free world."

Maurice didn't respond appropriately. He continued
his lecture: "The lifer soars into an elusive future or retreats
to his own time-locked island, where he is stranded, and
over time, stripped of hope."

"Shut it up, pal, I'm wide awake and living it now."

"Sorry, I get carried away."

"Ah, it's okay, just don't write a song about it."

"I won't."

"Good, the fear of not making it out of here has me
tied up in knots."

The professor didn't' know what to say, so he threw
up his hands, sat down and plucked the guitar to drive me
crazier.

2

I coughed to clear my throat and hacked up a deep-seated delusion Maurice's lecture stirred up: *Any second now, the guards will grab me, slap on shackles, and drag me back to the hole.*

But, at that moment, *Crash,* an old friend from *the Rock* came up behind me and placed a clammy hand on my shoulder. My body shuttered. "What in the world is wrong with you, Ninety-nine; I'm not the poleece!"

Moe snickered; I wheeled around and saw Crash's face. "Crash, you could have jammed my time!"

He giggled.

"Crash, you know not to rush up behind a convict...I could have..."

He interrupted me, "That's why they call me, Crash, I guess... but I didn't come over to jam your time: I came to share a dream I had last night."

Too wound up to hear what he had said, like an infant in his mother's arms, I waved loose hands at him and said, "Bye, bye!"

He smiled humbly, but held his ground. To apologize, I stretched out a firm hand and placed it on his shoulder. "Forgive me, you said something about a dream... if it's a good one, fire away!"

A serious look darkened his mug. I felt helpless, and without taking my eyes off Crash's face, plopped on the bunk beside Moe.

"It's a weird one about a man going home...you!"

I jumped up. "Wow, tell me about it!"

"I was in a smelly dorm like this one, except it had no windows and just one huge door. Like here, the place was stuffed full of guys in prison blue about ready to walk out the door on their way home."

"Sounds like a super dream." I enthused.

Crash continued. "It was; it may be a glimpse of something God wanted me to see, but I don't understand it. Ten or twelve men were lined up facing the door. As each one approached the exit, a correctional officer placed a small wooden cross in his hand."

I fidgeted, looked at Moe and said, "Well, I'll be."

"Each man's cross was a different size, and except for one, they were small enough to fit into the man's hand as he took it and high stepped it toward the door."

Moe stopped plucking, turned to Crash and said, "That's puzzling; I wonder why a cross, and why a C.O. handing them out?"

As a cloud came over his face Crash looked at me and said, "The officer thing makes no sense, but to me, it was a Christian cross like they gave us at Kairos, and it gets better now... I hope, for Ninety-nine."

"Go on; go on!" I said as I squirmed, twisted on the bed and grabbed Moe's Batman book. Crash eyed me, swallowed hard, and waited for me to settle down. I looked up at him and said, "Well, what happened next?"

"When your time came, the officer tried but couldn't place the cross in your hand."

Blood rushed to my face. "Why not?"

"It was too big...too heavy."

The image of a huge cross pressed heavy on my heart, but I choked out, "Could I carry it?"

"Well, kind of... you took hold of it and staggered toward the door, but that's when I woke up."

I slumped down on the bed, stared at the exit doorway in fear officers would descend on me at any moment. I gripped the comic book until Bat Man bled blue.

Moe must have seen the terror in my eyes and tried to ransom me with humor. "The heavy cross is this guitar."

It didn't work. I couldn't receive his humor and hung my head in despair, waiting for the guards to come.

Crash touched my shoulder and said, "Coop, it's going to be alright; you'll walk out a free man tomorrow, A.M."

I smiled at him but believed his nightmare rather than his words. I knew my doubts about getting out of prison were not misplaced...and my fears were not farfetched. Other men had been arrested at the gate and dragged back into lockup, their freedom stolen at the last moment. I had witnessed it. Besides, there were other banks; there were other crimes authorities could use to detain me and block my release. *They're coming to get me for sure. There's no way I'll walk... in the morning.*

In a daze I heard Crash tell me goodbye. I stood up and hugged him, but my heart wasn't in it. As he walked away, I turned and tossed Moe's crumpled comic book on the gray woolen blanket that served as a bedspread.

He picked it up, glanced at the cover that featured Batman in flight, cocked his head and peered at me with questioning eyes. "I ask you again...is this cross thing bothering you, Coop? You don't look like a man flying home."

Turning to him I said, "While you get that Batmobile tuned up, I'll make a quick pit stop back at the bat cave."

"Oh, no, you don't! I'm ready, now, Coop. I'm ready!"

"Hallelujah!" I yelled, not caring that my shout turned the head of the officer who was still making his rounds and caught the ears of inmates all around us.

Moe didn't care either. He smirked, strummed the chords and sang with a John Denver-soft tenor that blended with the guitar:

> *"The po-leece and the judges,*
> *The bankers, church members in the pews*
> *Are mumbling and grumbling,,*
> *Where is the justice? There's terrrrrible, terrrrrible bad*
> *news..."*

Moe's music was not amusing. To stop the music I stood up, stepped toward him, and raised my hands as if to attack him, but lowered them and said, "I like the melody, troubadour, but hate the lyrics...I've heard enough of this."

He guffawed. "You're right, my good homeboy, but *this* bad ballad may help you get ready for the harsh judgment coming your way."

His words cut deep. Not wanting to show it, I cocked my head and raised my eye brows, but didn't say a word.

He pointed a finger at me. "Don't expect a welcoming committee...many won't forgive you... or trust you ever again."

My gut tightened. *His words are true; some of the people, especially the victims, their family and my family: they're still hurting...still enraged. And they should be!*

His eyes became darts and his words daggers: "You'll have to be on your guard against cops and bankers."

12

I smiled a sick kind of smile, but still words wouldn't come. *I'm as tight as his guitar strings.* To loosen up, with both hands thrust deep into my pockets, I paced back and forth at a faster rate than before.

Moe followed me with his huge brown eyes, rose up and faced me.

I tried to stare him down, but finally, gave in, drew my hands out of my pockets and threw them into the air. "I've heard the exaggerated warnings about angry vigilantes."

Moe turned and checked to see if the officers were all in the control room from which they watched us. They were. He jumped up and with a swooping motion like that of an American History teacher erasing a blackboard with one long clean sweep of the eraser, he bellowed, "Beware, Coop! Beware! The bankers are coming; the bankers are coming!" Then, for the third time he defied the rules of the prison by straddling my cot where he mimicked a horseman bouncing atop a galloping horse.

Even for Moe, his raucous behavior stunned me. Nevertheless, I caught on to his charade, but his humorous antics took away my words. Finally, after about the fifth gallop, I managed to shout, "You mad man; you're Paul Revere!"

"You got it right, gentleman bank robber; you got it right," he bellowed.

Trying to tone things down, I snickered and snorted. In between gasps for air through fingers that covered my mouth, I said, "I may be... crazy, Paul Revere... but you are one... stark raving mad songwriter!"

13

With his goofy tirade, Moe had eased my fears I wouldn't make it out the gate, and he pulled me out of my funk. Eventually my sides hurt from cackling, but it felt really good to let my emotions come out through laughter.

"I know it, and I hope you will forgive me."

I caught my breath. "Paul Revere, from the back of this crazy horse galloping toward freedom's gate, it won't be easy."

He yelped like a happy puppy, shook my hand and said, "Good lyrics, my friend...yeah, my lyrics are mixed up a mite, but the bankers, if not the poleeece, and the people in the church pews may not be coming for you to snatch your freedom, but they will be lurking for you outside the gate, waiting for you to fly your true criminal colors. And don't forget this," he said with a stubby finger in my face, "they'll be coming to *welcome* you with their un-forgiveness!"

3

At nine the next morning, on the fourth day of June, I walked out the prison gate. No officer was stationed there to shackle me, hand cuff me or hand me a cross as Crash had envisioned, but when the heavy iron gate slammed behind me, like a wary stray dog, I glanced about to see if a guard from the pound lurked beyond the fences. Only one uniformed officer was in sight... a gruff looking one who waited for me to board the "Gray Goose" that would carry me to Dinsmore Work Release Center, the final freedom gate in Jacksonville.

I relaxed, exhaled the fear that had plagued me for days and inhaled the sweetest air I had breathed in a long time. Like a honey bee flitting from one sweet flower blossom to another I floated up the steps to board the bus. Inside, the stench of sweaty bodies brought me back to earth with an old gut-gnawing fear: *Going free is too good to be true!* But when the bus pulled out of the parking lot any remnant of paranoia was overcome by a feeling of euphoria: *I am free; this is the last prison bus I'll ever ride.*

Unlike trips in between prisons, this time I was allowed to board and ride without shackles or cuffs. The other nine passengers were also unshackled. From Lawtey, we headed north on U.S 301. A feeling of relief and freedom came over me, and I checked out what was happening through the heavily barred window of the bus that carried me away from internment. I couldn't see much through the web of iron but didn't care. The green trees, an occasional open place with a house, telephone poles along a railroad track, then a train whizzing by all spelled liberty for me.

I sighed. *The city of Jacksonville is only thirty-five miles to the northeast.* As the little prison community became small behind us, I thought about the time I spent at Lawtey CI with Moe: *I wonder if God put him there to prepare me for what lies ahead. Surely, the poleece and the bankers will not come out to "welcome" me as he predicted.*

In what seemed like an hour, we arrived at Dinsmore.

I looked around outside the modern looking facility. To my amazement, June Foster, a prison pen pal who had become a close friend during the final year of imprisonment, formed a one-woman welcoming committee. I wanted to hug her or at least say, hello, but a brusque looking officer marched me and the inmate brigade I was stuck in toward the glass doorway of the building. June stood to the side to allow us to enter, but managed to wave at me as I brought up the rear and was about to pass her. The radiance of her face reflected the joy of freedom that filled me up and overflowed. *She's an angel. Her eyes are wet with happy tears.* I paused long enough to say, "What a pleasant surprise!"

Her eyes sparkled. "Wouldn't be any..."

I didn't hear the last words as the door shut behind me, but figured the rest of the sentence was ...*where but here.* I smiled at that thought and said to myself, *wish her son Floyd was here, too.*

When the work release officer finished checking me in, he gave me permission to visit June. She waited for me in the reception area. When I stepped through the door she greeted me with a smile that lit up the lobby, open arms that lit up my heart and a huge shopping bag full of freedom clothes I would try on later. *I'm so thankful Floyd asked his mom to get me a set of street clothes.* Throughout the three minute special visit the officer allowed, everything fit perfectly...especially her embrace as we hugged goodbye and I whispered "until the next time."

After a three day in-house orientation by the staff that seemed like a month, I was driven around town in a smoke-filled prison van to look for work. I was dressed to the nines in my black suit and looked the part of the public relations executive I had been before my fall. *What a contrast to prison blues; except for smelling like a snuffed out cancer-stick, I could pass for the "gentleman bank robber."*

The interviews of the first three weeks brought nothing but turn-downs and disappointments. *The fact that I held high profile PR jobs is not a plus...their lips say they will call me but their eyes tell me the truth: they won't! They see me as a bank robber monster...not the gentleman I used to be. Moe was right. It will take a miracle for me to land a job in public relations. Imagine that.* I smiled and wondered what Moe was doing at Lawtey CI. I missed him and his guitar plucking more than I wanted to admit, but I surely didn't miss prison.

One steamy late June evening, on the way back to the work release center after another painful interview, I couldn't get my little buddy out of my mind. *If he could add a verse to his song it would include the rejection of employers. The media folks don't want to hire a forty-nine year old former gentleman bank robber so I'll look elsewhere.* At that thought tension left my body and I felt free for the first time in days. The self imposed stress dissipated.

Actually, the authorities who controlled my life were not pressuring me to find work immediately, so Dinsmore turned out to be exactly what was needed. They allowed me to ease back into society rather than hit the road running. And thanks to Jim Whyte, my sponsor from the Kairos Prison Ministry, I landed a job in the fourth week with The Florida Times-Union newspaper where he served as president and CEO. Jim's staff ignored my horrible typing speed of seventeen words a minute and hired me to write for the community news and features section called the *Neighbor*. I considered it a major miracle, and for me, each edition was a ransom note from God written by his grace.

By the end of the first month, as the work release center gave me a longer leash, June was allowed to pick me up from work. I loved the job but the joy of my life was June. Not only did we enjoy the rides back to Dinsmore, I spent most of my furloughs away from the community-based prison with her. Whether walking hand-in-hand on the beach, chasing clouds along the Atlantic seashore in her MGB convertible, or picking blackberries in a briar patch along the fences of Dinsmore, when we were together, the world around us disappeared. We were left alone to discuss our backgrounds, likes and dislikes... and in special moments, we compared life lines on our palms that "confirmed" a long bright future for us. From the day we met at Baker CI,, we believed God put us together for spiritual reasons...to organize and develop a ministry outreach called Adam (Adopt a Man) through which we would provide re-entry services to meet the transition needs of men coming out of prison, But as we got to know and love each other we wondered if God didn't have much more than a common ministry in mind for us.

One day when we held hands and said *Grace* before sharing lunch, the electricity that ran up my body, the excitement and yet comfort I felt in her presence, told me I had fallen in love with June. As I prayed I opened my eyes and beheld her beauty, the beauty of an innocent trusting child with her eyes closed, worshipping her heavenly father and reverently listening to me pray. In that moment it occurred to me that my focus was on her, not on God.

I closed my eyes, but still could "see" her elegant hair and smell a hint of alluring perfume. To keep from swooning, I squeezed her soft hand and concentrated on blessing the food she had prepared: "Dear Lord," I prayed, "I thank you for providing this food fit for a god"... and chuckled when I opened my eyes, surveyed the food set before us and said, "homemade chicken salad garnished with plump green grapes, English walnuts, surrounded by June's homemade bread and butter pickles..."

June withdrew her hand, chuckled and said, "Amen!"

I said, "Amen," pounded my fist on the table in jest, pointed at the huge crystal salad plate on the table between us and said, "surrounded by carrots, celery, cream dips and Brussels sprouts..."

Still amused, June exclaimed, "You're impossible!"

The little boy in me joined the little girl in her and said, "With God all things are impossible."

19

The glow on June's face reflected genuine joy, but her eyes became serious as she corrected me, "Possible, my good man...the word of God says with God all things are possible."

I took advantage of the opening and spouted, "I'm glad you agree, my dear, and hope that God agrees with me playing around a little bit while praying."

"I believe he's glad that you're happy and not afraid to show it...so enthused about chicken salad."

"A spread of food like this is impossible in prison."

June stared at the salad and said, "Mom says the way to a man's heart is through his stomach."

"Yeah, and through his eyes, ears and all the other holes in his head," I added.

"I sense that was a compliment," she said, smiling.

"Yes, your good cooking is surpassed only by your good looking."

She blushed, took the cellophane off the salad and said, "Let's eat this food before this high gets uglier."

I felt good, light-hearted as I grasped the truth that I liked everything about June from her good looks, sense of humor, faith, intelligence and chicken salad. I decided then and there I wanted to marry the woman sitting with me and spend the rest of my life with her.

When June left that day, for the first time, I kissed her passionately.

As I watched her drive away from the work release center in her just-right black sports car, the thought occurred to me how perfect it would be for me to propose to June in exactly the right way... at the most romantic time and place.

I know, I'll ask her to marry me on a date that has the number 7 in it... Some of the Bible teachers in the joint taught me that 7 in the scriptures stands for "God's perfection for man"...fantastic! June will perfect me, complete me, so seven months out of prison, on January 27, at 7:27 p.m. I'll ask June to marry me.

As I skipped back into the center, I giggled like a love struck teen age Romeo who had just conjured up the perfect plan to win the hand of his Juliette.

4

The moment on that late January day could not have been more romantic. A stream of blue and gold lights reflected off the bridges of the St. Johns River that connects and defines downtown Jacksonville. The skyscrapers lining the riverbanks witnessed our betrothal, but the words of proposal did not come easily. Fidgeting with the cold coins in my pocket reminded me of my cash shortage to start up married life with June, and a burst of frigid winter wind off the river caused me to question if this was the right time to ask her to marry me. A displaced ex-convict who hadn't yet proven himself worthy of being loved much less capable of providing for a woman once married to an heir of the Alka-Seltzer fortune. *I could surely use one right now, but June rejected his money at the divorce.* .

Despite these rapid fire thoughts, the beauty and romance of the moment prevailed. I took June's hand in mine. My heart thumped. *Robbing banks didn't make me this nervous,* I thought.

"Your hand is cold, Ken?' I winced. With every pulse beat, a fear of rejection heightened and my mind raced. *I'm used to it; nobody loves a convict thief...I certainly don't, but June is different; she has suffered like one of us rejects though she doesn't deserve it and she did day-for-day with her son, Floyd, in the joint.*

Finally, I managed to say, "I want to talk to you about something..."

A perplexed look on her face said, *"Oh, no, here it comes,"* but she said, "With sign language?" and smiled coyly.

Her beaming face encouraged me. Though I knew I could trust her, the fear of a negative response caused me to proceed with caution. It was one thing to admit to myself that she had captured my heart, but before asking for her hand in marriage, I sidestepped and said. "Sometimes I come down here to this very spot and talk to the river."

She squeezed my hand. "What does Mr. St. Johns River talk to you about?"

I pointed toward the silver black river as it rippled by and said, "See our distorted illusionary figures in the river's reflection. He told me y*ou are not a figment of my imagination."*

To continue the flow of the conversation, June waved at the St. Johns and said, 'I'm surprised a river would use a word like *figment.*"

"He said it to tease me about imagining what it would be like if you were not here with me," I said as I placed my arm around her shoulder.

At five feet five, she snuggled perfectly into the shelter of my arm. "No amount of figments or imagination could conjure up that picture," she whispered.

"I love being with you and I look forward to getting to know your parents better," I responded in her ear.

The woman I was going to ask to marry me cut to the chase: "They'll come around...they don't see you as a mobster or a monster."

I pulled away and said, "I must be to them; your parents don't want me to even date you."

"They don't know you like I do."

"No, but who can blame them? An ex-convict bank robber, I'm branded for life."

June reached out to me, squeezed my hand with one hand, pointed at my forehead with the other and declared, "I don't see a number on your forehead."

I pointed at seagulls that had gathered overhead at the river's edge, and said, "Honey, I'm overwhelmed to be out of that horrible place, but I still have to answer with my prison number when I'm counted each night."

"What do you mean by that?"

My emotions took over and I became melodramatic: "Given a life sentence - a grudge sentence of ninety-nine years- the state expected me to die at *the Rock*; so they make sure I'm on my bed and accounted for every night...but here I am with you on this beautiful river, without a number on my head, free as those sea gulls swooping down to count me."

June put her hands on her hips, looked at me like Mrs. Evenandahl, my third grade teacher and said, "I didn't know birds could count."

I joined her game and said, "Oh yes, they can since I'm not really free like them...yet."

"Ken, just like the sea gulls, you're a noisy mess."

"I know. Wish I could fly like them...going to work during the day and returning to lockup at Dinsmore to spend the night – it's like I've got one foot in a cage and one foot out; because of the Department of Corrections number carved on my forehead."

24

She knew what I was talking about. One rifle shot through two walls in her home changed her life forever. "Don't forget what I went through. When the accident happened, I lost one son to death...the other became a number in prison; most people turned their backs on me."

"Like you had committed a crime!"

"Exactly. But, maybe they just didn't know how to relate to me in my grief."

I put my arm around June's shoulder. "You lost two sons; it had to be impossible for you."

"A big part of me died... and I felt so alone. My friends seemed to disappear. When I ran into some of them who did Little League with us, or knew us at school, spotting me, they would shake their heads and back away without saying a word."

I dabbed a tear and said, "That added to your loneliness and hurt."

"It did, and yet in some ways, it was the best thing. I didn't know if I were coming or going, and let's face it; those people didn't know what to say to me."

"But you needed to talk to someone... anyone."

"Since there was no gentleman bank robber to talk to, I should have come down here and talked to the river."

"Old Man River would have kept your confidence better than that robber guy, for sure."

June covered her mouth with a hand and said, "Thank God I could trust the Lord and talk to Him, but I learned one thing: it's good to talk to a human being, a real friend about the person you've lost. Death is bad enough, but to never talk about your lost loved one, to remember the good times, or what they meant to you, is certainly worse."

I released her hand and stepped back so she could see my face. "You had to live with death, and at the same time, with the stigma of having a son in prison. That's too much to bear, especially when people treat you like an outcast."

I plopped down on a bench beside the river and June joined me. "Ken, in some ways, it's the same for you."

"What do you mean?"

"A lot of people will not know how to relate to you; they've never seen a bank robber, much less talked to one."

"And even fewer have kissed one of them varmints," I said as I leaned over and kissed her lips softly."

"You're impossible, sir- I'm being serious."

"That was a serious kiss!" I exclaimed.

My lady sneered and then forced a cough, but remained on track. "Like I said, you're open with me about your feelings and struggles, but most people don't know or don't care that you've been in prison.

I touched my forehead with three fingertips, and started to speak, but June's words flowed first. "Really, there's no number on your forehead," she said as she replaced my fingers with her own and brushed them across my forehead.

"I know; I know, but I feel like they are there."

She turned and faced me. "Oh, now I see it! It is a big Number *1*. Right there in the middle of your forehead," my lovely lady said, a look of mischief in her eyes.

I winked, took June in my arms and kissed her again.

Then, with our lips barely touching, I breathed, "I love you, Number One!"

"You are my *Number One,* too... I love you." she whispered.

Again, words wouldn't come from my heart. June's body tensed as she broke the silence, "But today's January 27, so you have 27 days and a wakeup before you walk out of that work release place."

I snorted and tossed my head like a horse galloping through the barn door, but myself, *I'll be free; June will say, yes; she's talking our numbers without even knowing it.*

But to my bewildered beloved, I said, "February 24 is my release date from Dinsmore, the last phase of prison for me, and work release gobbled up seven months of my life in half way lockup after three years in hard core prison."

"Yeah, but like you were saying, work release is hard time too, half way free is hard to deal with," June said.

I looked at June and thought about her approach to life and personality. She was the perfect woman for me; she knew prison, what it was like to be locked up because Floyd had served two years and was still doing time at Baker Correctional. A year earlier when I met June at Baker, we discovered that we had the same vision for our lives and even called it by the same name, *Adam:* Adopt a Man coming out of prison and help him adjust to life beyond the fences.

Knowing God had put us together for His purpose, I thanked him for leading me to my *Eve.* I held her in my arms and gazed over her shoulder at the black water laced with silver and gold taffeta, moon beams dancing on the mighty St. Johns.

But by this time my thoughts and our conversation had carried us downstream from the romantic course, so I asked the river, *"What would Floyd tell me if he were here? He introduced me to his mom at the visiting park in prison and has encouraged our relationship, so I know he approves. But would he tell me to wait, or ask his mother to marry me now?"*

The river didn't answer me, but when I turned around and gazed into June's eyes, they answered my question with a resounding *"Now!"*

At that moment, my self-confidence soared, and I kissed her full on the lips. Then, as envisioned for weeks, at 7:25 I took her hand like a gentleman would and guided her gently away from the river to the magnificent Friendship Fountain where at 7:27 I would ask her to marry me. The setting was perfect as we stood before the grand water cascade that graces the south bank of the St. Johns River.

At 7:27, when the majestic fountain shot thirty-foot water spouts into the evening air, it created a magnificent spray in the evening lights. We were caught up as one.

In the mist, the fountain lights formed countless tiny rainbows. *What an unusual breathtaking sight! Now I know what to say to June.*

June looked up toward heaven and beamed. I lowered my hands and drew her close. Her soft body melted into mine. I whispered into her ear, "Today, my love, I'm changing the name of this place from Friendship Fountain to Loveship Fountain."

"I can't imagine why," she said with a deep sigh.

Then she stepped back and her gorgeous blue eyes formed two question marks that seemed to taunt me, daring me to ask the big question.

So I did. But like my father before me, when he proposed to my mother, I knelt on one knee, and blurted "June, will you marry me?"

Her face flushed and her eyes lit up. But for a moment that seemed like an eternity, she stood in silence.

Captivated, I waited.

Finally, she formed words as if in slow motion and said, "Uh huh."

I laughed so hard I lost my balance and almost fell into the fountain. "What did you say?"

"Yes! I said, yes!"

"You did not. You said, 'Uh Huh.'"

"Ken, my thought was to say, no," she explained as she lowered her eyes.

Before I could react, she looked up and said, "But my heart made it come out that way."

I lifted my hands toward the sky and said, "I Thank God for that." To myself, I said, *June is mine!*

I rose up from my knees to kiss my betrothed. But when I stood before her, she pulled her body back enough to gaze up into my eyes. "Ken, I do love you; I want to be your wife...you'll be a good husband."

We kissed and held each other for a long moment out of time, knowing we were coupled for eternity.

5

What seemed like months later, but only thirty days after that, as "perfection" would have it, at seven p.m. Friday, February 27th, we were married at the home of Ken and Clara Power, Kairos friends who ministered to me in chapel services at the Rock. The wedding ritual was held under their poolside gazebo. Despite the absence of June's parents, her son Floyd, the Cooper clan, including my daughter, Becky, it was a glorious, sacred marriage ceremony officiated by Reverend Barry Myers, a volunteer chaplain from Baker Correctional. My best man was Jim Whyte.

Though tremendously blessed to have them standing with me, and though my old buddy Moe stood before me smiling ear to ear in the throng of radiant witnesses, as I waited for the ceremony to begin, I felt alone. I missed my mother and brothers, especially my beloved Becky, who couldn't make it from Louisville because of her husband, three kids and work demands. I figured the rest of the family had equally good reasons for not being there, but still their absence hurt.

When it was time for the wedding march to play, though, it comforted me that I stood between two men of faith who accepted me despite my criminal past. Chaplain Barry had become a spiritual guide, and I was honored that a person of Jim's dignity and stature would stand up with me. I looked at the tall debonair Irishman, flashed a smile, and expressed my gratitude, forcing gravelly words out of the corner of my mouth like a gangster, "Thanks Irish Jim, I feel like a jail bird set free."

"It's too late now to fly, Clyde; *this* is a life sentence of another sort," he retorted.

I grinned and whispered, "Yeah, with God's blessing, Bonnie and I will serve a life time together..."

Jim hushed me with a motion of his hand and pointed toward the back door of the Power's home. I stopped the nervous chatter. My eyes followed his finger down a candle-lit poolside that formed a bright path for the wedding procession. Floyd's wife, Cherrie, June's matron of honor, appeared in the doorway, ready to begin her walk toward us, and their three-year-old, June Carlene, stood behind in the doorway.

My mind raced. *How I wish Floyd were here, wish my sweet Becky and her family had come down from Louisville. She could have sung at our wedding.*

I glanced at Cherrie. Deep gratitude coursed through my being. *Becky and this gorgeous daughter-in-law will get along great, and my three grand kids and the precious little lamb named June Carlene, disguised as a flower girl.*

At that moment, the wedding march sounded, Cherrie walked down the aisle and June Carlene took her first dainty step and traipsed along behind her mother tossing rose petals into the air that fluttered like pink butterflies onto the deck and into the placid water that reflected their beauty.

I thought out loud, "How absolutely beautiful, peaceful...perfect; what a stark contrast to prison!" I dabbed a tear and pushed back the thought that I didn't deserve a family, much less this kind of happiness.

The pink petals on the wooden deck formed a pathway for my beloved. I shuffled on anxious feet and sweat dampened both palms. My bride would soon appear.

A moment later, when the Bridal March sounded on an organ behind me, June came into view and started down the aisle. My heart stopped. Her radiance drew me, and the distance between us vanished. She appeared absolutely stunning, perfect in a three tiered light pink gown, a dark pink hat over a white veil, with a bouquet of white and pink roses in her hand. I wondered if this was how Adam felt the first moment he saw Eve.

Then I noticed her escort, Lindsay, my good friend and roommate at Dinsmore. Standing in for Floyd, Lindsay beamed and appeared to be as proud as if he were June's son.

But I only had eyes for June, and before I knew what had happened, she stood before me. I heard Chaplain Myers speaking as if from a distance, "Who gives this woman to be married?"

"I do in behalf of her son, Floyd," Lindsay declared with his best tenor voice as he released June.

My bride stepped forward. We took right hands and turned to face the Chaplain. I floated through his first words, but settled down to repeat our wedding vows and slip on the rings. When he pronounced us husband and wife, I lifted the bridal veil from June's lovely face and sealed our promises with a passionate kiss.

I heard tittering laughter and applause; Chaplain Meyers introduced us as Mr. and Mrs. Ken Cooper, and we stepped out of the gazebo into the beaming crowd. It overwhelmed me that fifty people, mostly Kairos Prison Ministry volunteers, came to celebrate with us. I was especially pleased to see June's brother, Douglas, his wife Diane, and their family.

But receiving congratulations from Christian brothers I served time with at *the Rock* brought tears. Of course, the first to greet June and me and set the tone was Maurice and his wife, Eve. They were also newlyweds and their glow showed it though my parole officer had not granted permission to attend their wedding out of county in Ocala a month earlier..

Following hugs that hurt my ribs, June and I stood with them, sipping punch when I acted as though I was fainting so my old buddy from prison would be forced to catch me.

As he caught me and held me in his arms, in his best Moe impersonation, Maurice said, "Come on Coop; you knew we'd *fall* for beautiful creatures of God."

"Unless we died in prison first, Moe; except for Becky's regular visits, your songs and prayers, I wouldn't be here."

"I'm sure glad she visited you before God healed us of our leprosy 'cause we'd still be *there*," he said, pointing west in the general direction of the five state prisons some forty miles away.

I rubbed the top of his hand and said, "Unclean, unclean!!"

We all groaned at the sick joke and drew closer.

I took June by the hand, looked at her, glanced at Eve and said, "Maurice and I shared a vision while still in *the Rock*. When God has humbled us to the point that we are the best husbands in Florida, we'll return as ex-convict ministers, he'll do the singing; I'll do the preaching; please pray for us and yourselves, dear wives...cause you'll go with us."

Before anyone could respond, a photographer came up, posed us for a picture and then dragged June and me off for a shot with other friends.

Moe and Eva moved along behind us. In between snapshots he tapped me on the shoulder and looked at June: "Your marriage vows said nothing about going to prison?"

I held up June's hand and retorted, "June, I'll be your prisoner till death do us part."

The four of us snickered, shook hands, hugged again, and separated to mingle with the crowd. As June and I celebrated our marriage, and I felt the love of well wishers, joy filled me once more to overflowing like it had upon my arrival at freedom's gate at Dinsmore. The love and acceptance of our friends washed away my shame and self condemnation. For the first time in weeks, I forgot about my crimes, I forgot about the victims; I forgot about prison; I forgot about everything but my bride and our moment.

When Jim Whyte led the gathering in a toast, he raised his glass and with a sparkling Irish tenor voice he saluted us: "May God continue to bless you, Ken and June. May His face shine upon your marriage, and may you fulfill your destiny!"

34

His beautiful *Southern Belle*, Doris, beamed and I acknowledged the magnificent toast with my glass held high, glanced at June and pointed toward heaven to give the credit to God. She did the same with her left hand, our wedding ring sparkling in the light. When she lowered her hand and held a wine glass high with in her right hand, I realized it made her look like the Statue of Liberty. I smiled at that beautiful picture of freedom.

One of my favorite traditions, the cutting of the wedding cake, came next. Doris Whyte had furnished a three tiered white cake masterpiece of sculpted white icing for the ceremony. June and I used a silver spatula, each placing a right hand on the shining handle, as we cut two pieces of cake. We then each held a piece in preparation for feeding our faces. June's stern eyes told me that I had better not give in to the urge to stuff too much into her mouth. She was six inches shorter, but her look told me I would wear a tall amount of cake if I gave in to the temptation. That moment became my first opportunity to acquiesce to my wife. So I used great care in placing a mannerly slice in her mouth. The moment was sweet, and I realized caving in to this woman might be a good thing and something that would happen quite often.

At the end of the evening, when we rushed through the rice gauntlet, love pellets stinging my face and neck, I felt truly loved by June and by our new *family*. When we arrived at the escape vehicle, however, darts of regret pierced me: my brothers hadn't been there to soap up the car and tie on the tin cans. And I missed my mom.

35

A moment later when we drove away in my little Escort station wagon, I shouted over the clatter of the noise of tin can tag-alongs trailing us, "Hey Bonnie, this is definitely not quiet enough to be our *getaway car.*"

"I love the rattling tin cans, Clyde, and I'm grateful Ken and Clara helped you get this wagon."

"It's just right for our new beginning."

Something rattled off the seat. I looked down and spotted a box of Cracker Jacks on the floorboard. Like an eight year old, I begged June to open the box and make it our first meal. She must have read my mind or guessed what I was really after: the prize inside. She pillaged the caramel corn until she found it. My bride smiled and said, "You're nothing but a big kid, my husband."

The surprise was a little plastic banner inscribed with two letters, *B-C.* We looked at each other in astonishment and exclaimed, "Bonnie and Clyde!!"

"Can you believe it?" I said, chortling.

We joked about it and vowed to haul Bibles in the back of our "Cadillac" rather than stolen loot from banks. I placed two fingers on the dashboard and dubbed the little guy, *B.C.* "From this time forward, little friend, you will be known as *B.C.,* as in Bonnie and Clyde."

6

Two hours later, when we arrived at a Palatka motel, fifty miles south of Jacksonville, I carried June across the threshold of the room where we would spend our first night. It had been booked by Floyd and Cherrie. In fact, it was their wedding gift. Prior to his going to prison, they were married in Palatka at Cherrie's mother's home and spent their first night there. With big smiles and bright eyes they told us, "It's a really cool place; you'll enjoy it."

When my lovely bride's feet touched the floor inside the door, however, she glanced around and began laughing. Her laughter surprised me, and I looked up to see what struck her. I couldn't believe my eyes. We were standing on the edge of an enormous playroom with mirrors covering all four walls and the entire ceiling. Across the room from us beckoned an immense Jacuzzi that took up one wall. A whopper sized waterbed occupied the heart of the playroom, and over it, a swing dangled from a rope stretched tight between two walls. A trapeze ran from a pulley above a closet door and crossed the room to a "launching pad" over the bed.

"Can you believe this!" I exclaimed and pulled myself up onto the swing.

"You wouldn't dare, Ken."

I beat my chest and did my best Tarzan scream.

June smirked and retreated to the Jacuzzi. My eyes followed her to the blue manmade swimming hole shaped like a crescent. I leaped off the swing, bounded across the bed, eased over behind her and pulled her body to mine. She turned and we kissed as only newlyweds can kiss.

My next move did not surprise her. Motioning toward the bed, I said, "Honey, let's..."

My wife interrupted me, "Suits me, Tarzan, as long as you stay off that swing."

We snuggled into bed and became Adam and Eve on their first night in Eden. But it turned out that sleeping on a waterbed wasn't our idea of paradise. Nevertheless, tossing and sloshing, Friday evening became Saturday morning and we slept late.

After breakfast in the room, we shared a devotional from Robert H. Schuller's *Daily Power Thoughts*, the book I used throughout my prison stint. The theme for the day was *Today I Begin Anew*. We glanced at each other in shock when we read the title. It fit our situation perfectly.

I shared Dr. Schuller's words with June.

"The theme for the week is Hope. Everywhere I go I meet people who tell me, 'My life has been changed.' And it is because there is change that there can be hope. Whatever your circumstances are today, it will change. Tomorrow will be different. And the amazing thing is that you can choose how your tomorrow will be different."

"It's certainly the right word for today, our first day," June said.

"I must be open with you," I responded.

"Ken, you look as if you're down; what's troubling you?"

"My life has been changed, thanks to Jesus coming into my heart and God putting you in my life," I told her, "But I'm anxious about the future."

"Ken, what in the world are you concerned about?"

"You've seen some of the stuff I'm going through; the flashbacks, getting readjusted to life out here. I hope you'll put up with me."

"You know I will, honey, as long as you stay away from waterbeds and banks."

I chuckled. My new wife's sense of humor had a way of making things better, but I said, "That's exactly what I'm talking about; I'm labeled a bank robber everywhere I go."

"Really, most people have never met a bank robber, so there's a certain mystique, a curiosity..."

My face must have told her I wasn't happy with her attempt to encourage me. She touched my arm, and said, "They won't know unless we tell them."

"But you see, my dear, that's the problem, everywhere I go, that's how people introduce me. They say it in a lighthearted or joking way... especially in the churches or groups when pastors ask me to share my testimony."

Again, June tried to lighten things up. "I won't mind being your Bonnie."

"I know you're with me; I just want to handle the stigma better."

She put her arms around me. "Consider this Mr. Bank Robber. It may simply be God's purpose for your life. He wants people to know he can change anybody. He wants you to tell people how God released a guy like you from prison real early so he could change others through you."

"Yeah, I'm amazed to be free: less than four years on ninety-nine, wow!"

"People will see you have changed, and He will get the glory for it."

"I don't mind baring my soul and sharing my testimony; I just wish it was better for you. Your parents..."

June placed two fingers on my mouth, stopped my words and said, "I'm here to support you."

I smiled. Words were not necessary.

Like we had done the evening before when we said our vows, we stood face-to-face. This time, however, we joined outstretched hands and began to pray. June stood silently while I spoke out loud, "Lord, I thank you that you gave me the perfect wife, one who loves you and me with all her heart and is willing to help me during these coming days and months as I get used to being back on the streets. We thank You for this day and return it to you as an offering."

Accustomed to talking with God alone, but new at praying with a second person, it occurred to me June might want to pray, too, so I hesitated. When she didn't pick up the cue, I continued, "And father right now I promise to end each of our daily devotions with the *Prayer of St. Charles...*"

The reference to the *Prayer of St. Charles* caught June by surprise. To interrupt me and ask what it was about, she squeezed my hand firmly enough to hurt my ring finger, but she remained silent. I flinched and said "Owh!...Amen!"

June looked up into my eyes, "Before you pray that prayer – what did you call it – the Prayer of St. Charles? Tell me about it... who is Charles... first."

I said. "Babe, this is kind of far out, or maybe I should say *far in.*"

My wife of ten hours looked puzzled.

40

"When I was a brand new Christian in jail, I asked the Lord to send a man of God, a strong Christian, to help me. I was in the worst cell in the Hillsborough County Jail where rape was happening every night. A brand new Christian, I didn't know if God would put a stop to it, but I figured it made sense to ask him to, but I didn't know how to pray."

June said, "Go on."

"Well, the man God sent to pray with me would certainly not have been my choice for a prayer partner. The cell mates and I thought he was crazy, and he probably was, but he really believed in God and knew how to pray.

June leaned toward me and listened intently.

"Charles slept with his eyes wide open. He talked to angels and even called them by name. And if you called him by anything but Charles, including his last name, Johnson, he would punch your lights out!"

June formed a fist to show her amusement, but asked, "He was a crazy kind of character, wasn't he?"

"Yeah, but I learned that just because you're crazy doesn't mean you can't be a Christian."

She laughed and said. "And just because you're a Christian doesn't mean you can't be crazy."

I laughed with my beloved, but remained serious. "Well, Charles taught me a far out thing about prayer; he showed me in the Bible that God wants us to ask the Lord to involve His angels in our lives."

My bride looked puzzled, so I continued, "I'd never heard of such a thing either, but Charles told me he based his prayers on a scripture from the first chapter of Hebrews, a passage about how God sends his angels to minister *for* us."

"You mean they will actually minister *for* us as well as *to* us?"

"That's right. But as I learned from Charles, we must pray and in faith thank God in advance for sending them if we really want them to be active in our lives."

"Okay, okay, I know you're far out, Mr. Preacher Man, but before I fall out from standing here so long, I'm ready to hear this St. Charles' prayer."

I thanked my new wife for her patience and for believing in me. I closed my eyes and talked to God. "Father as I have done these past years, I ask you to send your angels to work behind the scenes with your Holy Spirit to help bring about your perfect will in our lives that we, and each person we pray for this day, shall be in the right place at the right time with the right word with the right people for your right purposes. Amen."

June said she was really impressed with the prayer and could hardly wait to see how God used His angels to place us in the right place at the right time with the right people. I told her I didn't expect it to happen that day or even on our honeymoon trip, but I hoped it would.

7

To my delight, God's heavenly intervention happened in about two hours, on the second jaunt of our honeymoon trip as we drove toward the Epcot Center near Disney World. It was early afternoon, and we decided to stop at the next restaurant we came to and treat ourselves to an ice cream sundae. About that time I spied a McDonald's, pulled in and parked. In the joint I'd heard they served great sundaes.

Though we were both forty-nine, we strolled in like young lovers, hand-in-hand, toward the west entrance of the restaurant. A youthful mom and dad with three little kids smiled at us as we passed. Their beaming faces told me they knew we were in love, but I didn't care. I felt so complete, alive from the top of my head to bottom of my feet. But when we walked through the door, I almost dropped dead. Darkening the portal across the lobby was one of my closest friends from Dinsmore Work Release Center in Jacksonville.

"June, look, look; it's Michael Hamm!"

She laughed and pointed a finger toward the ceiling. I knew what she was thinking. Michael was two-hundred miles from home. The chances were astronomical we would see the one person I knew in Orlando – at a McDonald's. God had answered our prayer and apparently used his angels to put us in the right place at the right time with the right person.

I threw up my hand and yelled across the room to get Michael's attention. His face lit up and he yelled back, "What in the world are you doing here in Lake Mary?"

"June and I had nothing better to do than hook up with you!"

He glided across the floor toward us like he had wings. June looked on as we embraced as only ex-convicts who have served time together can.

I took June by the hand and said, "June, you remember Michael from Dinsmore."

"Sure, he tried to talk you into sharing some of the potato salad I brought to the visiting park."

"Hi, June, I hope you have taught Ken to share by now."

June's face beamed. "Now it seems like he's hung up on ice cream."

"That's enough, you two; I know you're after my sundae, but it ain't going to work."

With joy on our faces we moved outside, sat on a grassy knoll overlooking the area, and enjoyed our treats as we talked. I told him about the Prayer of St. Charles and that our meeting at that McDonald's was a good example of how God used His angels to put us together.

"I believe that," he said without batting an eye.

"Maybe it takes faith on both ends to make it work," June interjected.

"I'm not sure about that, but I do know this. I passed by this place, but an inner voice told me to turn around and come back. I listened to the urge, but wondered about it because I really don't like McDonald's hamburgers."

"They sure do make good sundaes," I said, deep chocolate on my lips punctuating each word.

"God must have stopped me for this meeting, Coop... this is a strange way to meet," he said.

As I listened to him talk I remembered the day I met him eight months earlier. Michael had impressed me with his energy and faith. The sidekick and pilot for Jack "Murf the Surf" Murphy, the world class surfer and notorious Star of India Sapphire thief turned minister, Michael had just returned from an evangelistic tour with his old pal from Raiford.

Finally, I responded to him and said, "I believe God sent you with a message..."

Michael interrupted me by laughing loudly. He raised a finger and pointed toward the sky. Then, he announced with an exaggerated bravado, "I'm an arc angel sent by God."

June and I looked at each other and disbelief lit up her face.

Michael continued. "It's clear to me God put you together for His sake and for the sake of men coming out of prison."

"How's that?" I asked.

"God never wastes anything, our good experiences, what we consider bad; He uses it all to prepare us for what He wants us to do in life."

June and I nodded our heads in agreement, then I said, "When June and I met in prison, we had the same vision and even called it the same thing, *Adam,* Adopt a Man and help him adjust to life outside the prison fences."

45

"That's a fantastic thing; there is no greater need," he said, and added, "I'd like to do the same thing some day."

I smiled and said, "Well, you can practice on me and my needs to get us both started."

June's bright look let me know she understood, but Michael's brow was plowed with deep questions. He asked, "What's your needs got to do with it?"

"How in the world could I meet the needs of other men coming out? I'm having real problems adjusting myself."

"Well, now Coop, that's a good thing because you'll be a wounded healer who will be able to help ex-cons cope with the same stuff you are going through."

Embarrassed, I looked at June and smiled. She said, "Experience is the best teacher."

"You're both right on, but there are several things bothering me I'd like to talk about," I said.

"Fire away," Michael said, leaning toward me.

"You've been out for several months now, so I want to pick your brains."

"Six to be exact."

"Brains, or months?" I asked trying to lighten the mood.

"I never have been very smart, just blessed," he said.

I looked at June, got her approval with a nod, and said to Michael, "I'm having a harder time getting adjusted out here than I expected."

"Like, what's bugging you?" he asked.

"I'm extremely blessed to be out in three years on ninety-nine, but I'm hamstrung by a feeling of unworthiness, imminent doom in nightmares back in prison...fear..."

"All kinds of fun stuff," he said, teasing.

"I have a hard enough time loving myself enough to expect the blessings of God, so the fear of being arrested for other banks, the feeling the rejection of others may bother me more than most."

"Whoa, boy, whoa. Let's take em one at a time."

I held my hand out and said, "I'll slow down, I really need to talk about these gut things.

Michael nodded that he understood, looked me in the eye and said, "Ken, I know it's natural for you...for all of us to want everyone to love us, but it just ain't that way out here for anybody, much less for ex-convicts."

I looked at June, smiled and said. "I know."

He continued, "In between trips with Murf, I've spoken in several churches already, sharing my testimony as the pastors ask me, but it seems to split the believers right down the middle."

"What do you mean?" June asked.

"The church members are divided; some of them love me, but most of them can't, and I feel it."

"Wow, that's heavy," I said.

"For sure, brother; be ready for people to judge you and have difficulty accepting you as one of them."

I remembered Maurice's prediction of rejection my last night in prison and said, "I'm surprised people in the churches can't believe a bank robber can change."

My ex-convict friend laughed. "Hey, man, you know the scriptures: God blesses us weak ugly rejects and promises us the Kingdom of Heaven to confound the wise and

47

teach them that the foolish things of God are wiser than the wisdom of men."

My tendency was to hide or ignore my weaknesses, and I was not ready to face the truth, so I changed the subject: "I expected people out here to be different," I responded.

June motioned to Michael, looked me square in the eyes and said, ""You always look for the best in yourself and others; people, even church members do not think that way and can be very cruel. I'm concerned already for Floyd when he comes out."

I squeezed her hand, relieved the conversation had taken a turn away from me.

Michael interjected, "I don't know him, June, but with the support of you two, he should do fine."

"Oh, I know he will; it's just a mama thing."

"That-a-girl, *Mrs.* Cooper, with the Lord's help, both husband and son will be just fine."

"Thank you, Michael; I like being called Mrs. Cooper, especially when you're talking about our family being blessed."

Michael stood up and looked toward the parking lot for his car. We had been talking for an hour. "Well, now, you love birds, I'll let you fly away to your nest while I go fry some other fish."

"Thanks for your good words and lead us in prayer before you head out, my friend," I said as we joined hands.

Michael prayed, "Father we thank you for our freedom, and I thank you for putting me with Ken and June today for your reasons. Please take all fear from us that we may trust you more. Amen!"

When I opened my eyes Michael was staring at me. "There's one last thing," he said, leaning back, then tilting his head forward to hold my eyes with his. "You have taken a stand as a Christian called to help others, so expect this test to continue."

I stepped away and released my grip on his hand. "Like you've said, hopefully, as weak as I am, the Lord Jesus will be even stronger, so perhaps I'll be ready someday," I told him.

A few days later, when the next big test came, I wasn't ready.

8

Home from our honeymoon, I returned to work on Monday morning. Stepping out of *BC*, my feet were light on the pavement, and as I approached the Times-Union building, my long shadow skipped along like a man on stilts dancing with the rising sun. After a few paces, I looked around to see if anyone was watching, and continued to dance toward my work place. I felt so good.

Right away, though, as I stepped into the building a feeling that things weren't right came over me. The warning was confirmed the moment I walked into the community news section. Not one of the three writers at their work stations acknowledged me. And their body language told me they had just been talking about me. I figured my typing seventeen words a minute on a good day had caught up with me and I was about to be fired as a staff writer. I sat down at my computer and said, "Good morning!"

John, the staff writer who sat next to me, swiveled in his chair and said, "Good morning, Ken, we need to talk to you."

His serious tone and stern face reminded me of my first grade teacher. I tried to hide the little boy in me with a smile. "What's up?" I asked.

He leaned back, waved a hand above his head and said, "Jim, Sarah and I have been talking, Ken, and we want to clear the air about a certain rumor."

My heart dropped into my gut and a slight adrenalin rush kicked in. "What's up guys?" I asked, trying to hide my anxiety with a cheerful tone.

John responded, "We like you, Ken, and have accepted you though you're a bank robber, but some disturbing word came through news sources."

I tried to maintain a light-hearted air: "Hey guys, that wasn't me that hit that downtown bank on Saturday."

All three laughed, but my reference to a bank robbery that occurred over the weekend didn't ease the tension.

John cleared his throat and said, "That would shock me, Ken, but no more than hearing that you took hostages when you robbed banks."

Tension gripped me. My mind couldn't receive his words and I wanted to crawl into a hole. I slumped into a stupor and stared at the floor.

Sarah, who sat on my right, broke the silence.

"It was bad enough when the editor told us at the staff meeting when she introduced you that the newspaper had hired a bank robber; this thing about taking hostages is more than shocking. I want to hear it's not true, before we get too upset."

Though a wave of shame engulfed me, I lifted my head and turned to face her. Her large gray eyes seemed to devour me as she waited for my response. I lowered my eyes, cleared my throat and tried to speak but nothing came out. On the second attempt, I managed, "What..uh...my main victims were women... what you've heard is true."

Her mouth dropped open. Waiting for Sarah to collect herself, I paused for a moment. I sensed there were no

51

words to help me out of the jam, so I let my emotions speak through my body. I held my hands up, with palms turned upward, and looked toward the ceiling to express my feelings of helplessness and surrender. Then, I said, "I don't know what to say, but one thing I can tell you is that I'll regret what I did to them and my family every day... the rest of my life."

"Then, it's true," Sarah said. The word *true* remained pursed on her lips.

"Yes, I'm so sorry; er...at times, there were women involved when I did a bank job."

A stark silence rose up like an ill wind and settled over us.

The wrong words, *women involved in a job*, had come out. I couldn't bring myself to say hostage or victim again, and I shouldn't have referred to my heinous crimes as a *job*. But I couldn't take my feeble explanation back, so I tried again, this time determined to tell the harsh truth. "What I mean is my main victims were women...er, I'd take a hostage to buy the time I needed to get away."

Sarah and Jim jumped up and stepped back into a cloud of indignation that darkened their faces. A sick grin widened my lips. *If condemnation could smother a man, I would suffocate.*

John stood up slowly and rescued me. "Listen," he said. "Appears to me Ken has told us the truth, bad as it is, let's give him a chance to show he has changed."

Neither of the writers responded so John continued, "After all, we're not his victims so he deserves that much."

Jim and Sarah plopped down in their chairs, and Jim asked, "If there was one, what was your turning point?'

His question opened a door for me. I forced a cough to clear my voice and said, "Six weeks before I was sentenced to serve ninety-nine years in lockup, I gave my life to God. That was in jail. Then, in a prison called *the Rock*, I was broken."

No one said anything but arms crossed in front of rigid bodies told me they had rejected my explanation. Like reporters should, they wanted to hear facts, rather than a testimony about my conversion, so I continued, "That was the beginning of my reformation, and I'm not a threat to ..."

John stopped my words with an upheld hand, leaned forward, touched my arm and said, "That's good enough for me, Ken. I'm willing to give you a second chance, and I hope everyone else will do the same."

Unable to concentrate on writing in the same room with my adversaries, and needing time to recoup, I made my way through a cloud of morose that had settled over me, staggered out the door and dragged my body over to the art department in the advertising section where my best friend and good buddy, John, worked.

"What's up with you, Coop...looks like you lost your best friend," said my pal who had also served time in prison but had been a free man for thirty years.

"You're right on, John, but you're my best friend...hopefully I haven't lost you," I said as I plopped on a work stool before a desk that held the day's art work for a full page ad by Nimnicht Chevrolet.

He grinned at me, turned to his masterpiece, pointed at a sleek red Corvette on the page and declared, "There's no way that a sport car like you can park in my garage and make that kind of noise."

I chuckled at his humor, but said, "I just left my computer...the writers who work with me...they don't want to be a bank robber's friend right now."

John looked up, held my eyes with his and said, "Coop, that old stinkin' thinkin' guy is behind you, but they're just now learning to live with your ugly past."

"You're right, John; that's exactly what came down when they found out I had taken women victims as hostages during some of the robberies," I said as I held my hands up in surrender.

"They'll come around; just give them time."

I chuckled, "As in prison time; it's been several months now and ..."

My friend interrupted me. "It took them ten years to love an ex-convict recluse like me, and some of the cynical types still don't," John said laughing.

I joined him and said, "Yeah, you're right. I've got to be patient."

"For sure, pal; you know the old saying. "You did the crime so you must do your time, Ninety Nine."

I laughed and said, "But I'm still doing it."

John ignored me and continued, "You've got ninety-five years and a wake up to go, pal," he said as he stood up and waved me away from his desk.

I didn't budge and said, "If you're talking about this Vette doing 95 MPH, I can handle that."

"You go slow, boy, you go slow; that's the key"

....

54

From that day on, while the two *Johns* treated me like friends, several staff members steered clear of me. In the days and weeks that followed, as word got around, I saw the big eyes of fear from a number of women staffers when they passed me in the hallways. It hurt me, but I understood their fear and prayed they would someday come to trust me. For the most part the men had less trouble accepting me and a few became friends like John, the artist, who continued to treat me like a brother.

To my surprise, the difficulty I was having with the majority didn't affect my production as a writer. In fact, my having less social contact with peers gave me more time to focus on writing to meet the editor's deadlines. I loved doing feature stories, but as the weeks became months, the stress of meeting deadlines and the continuing rejection by some of the staff caused me to withdraw from them and threatened to lock me up in a prison of my own making.

9

In August, to keep me from digging a deeper hole and plunging into a pit of depression like the ones I experienced in prison, June suggested I take a break from work and visit my mom in Kentucky.

"You mean like a jail break, Bonnie?"

"Yeah, that's what I mean, Clyde, and nobody's going to charge you with escape."

I thanked God for giving me a wife with a sense of humor and an understanding of my needs. "Moe warned me of PITS that last night in lockup."

"Remind me what the letters stand for."

I smiled but became serious: "Post Institution Trauma Syndrome."

"I know what it's about...the nightmares continue..."

I interrupted June: "Yeah, and the bloody flashbacks in the middle of a conversation...that kind of stuff."

June touched my shoulder. "Rise up, free man! Go enjoy your freedom!"

....

The next morning I skipped like Moe out the back door and pointed little *BC* toward Interstate-95, three miles east of our home in north Jacksonville. Though June couldn't go with me, I agreed that a change of pace could lift me out of the PITS and do me good. Besides, it was past time for me to go *home* for a quality visit with mom. Except for a quick stop in the spring to introduce my bride, I hadn't ventured up that way.

It was hard to leave June and the "I love you more than life" kiss we shared lingered until I crossed the Florida-Georgia state line some thirty miles north of the River City. *June was born in southwest Georgia...boy am I going to miss my Georgia peach.* But through the morning as *BC* and I headed for mother's home place in McCreary County, Kentucky, we could not have been happier. Though I missed June, a feeling of freedom formed a ten-hour tailwind that pushed my little Escort northward as we glided effortlessly across US 84 from Waycross to Tifton and up Interstate-75 through Atlanta into Tennessee at Chattanooga.

Two hours later, we had climbed from the foothills north of Knoxville to the top of the Cumberland Mountains that divide Tennessee and Kentucky, some two thousand feet above the Cumberland River valley floor.

I was "home" in the mountains and began to daydream about how the Cooper clan moved into Claiborne County Tennessee at Jacksboro a hundred fifty years earlier. I thought of Becky and her husband, Kenny Ellison, whose family also called Claiborne home. *Wow, I wish my Becky, Kenny, JP, Javonna and Lee were all crammed in with me, heading home.*

Waking out my "trip" it seemed that *BC* and I were moving along the mountain top trail as slowly as my ancestors had moved in horse drawn buggies and wagons. But still I marveled at the ridges that formed long links in the Appalachian chain that stretches from northern Alabama to Maine.

Suddenly the little station wagon and I topped a hill and plunged into a dense fog. My heart dropped into my gut which belched, *I'm in a cloud; I can't see a thing!* The heavy mist acted as a mirror that reflected the headlights back into my eyes. The glare blinded me and obscured the roadway. With the fog came a strange cloud of fear darkened by worry I hadn't felt since prison. I was afraid of crashing into something and dying, but an even greater fear welled up in my throat and choked me. *I'm scared to death of the unknowns that lie ahead.*

Straining to make out the roadway before me, I dreaded how family and friends would receive me. *I'm sorry I avoided them on the last trip, Father. Why am I so insecure? Please forgive me and help me to handle their rejection and my fear of the future.* In that moment of thinking, fear became so real that it seemed to settle into the seat beside me as my copilot. I slowed BC to a crawl. I missed June, my navigator. But rather than talking to *fear* I talked to my wife as if she were by my side. *Honey, I sure could use your presence, your eyes right now; hope you're praying for me!*

I was still driving blind, but expressing my emotions to June seemed to help me relax, and the morbid fear began to dissipate. At the same time, though it seemed impossible, the fog got thicker. It engulfed me and took me back to see the cloud of black fog that rolled toward me every night in mystifying nightmares that plagued me in *the Rock*. In each horrifying dream a woman would step toward me out of the dark haze with a terrified look on her face. As she came closer I could see her face of horror and her eyes of pain. But each time, when I extended my hands to reach out to her, the terrified woman disappeared into the night.

I shuttered, gripped the wheel and cried out to God: *"Oh, God, I know that she's my victims, the horrified women I took hostage during holdups; I'm so sorry. Please forgive me Lord; please comfort them and please allow me to reach out to them...somehow... when they're ready."*

The fog seemed to lift a little, but a blanket of insecurity still covered me so I continued crying out to God. *"Oh God, I deserve to die like this but it would be strange to get run over by a truck in this fog when I survived the Rock... I'd rather die facing my victims, the reporters, my family; I disgraced them, but I wish Dad were alive. He'd make a great co-pilot."*

I laughed at that reassuring thought and suddenly out of the fog, up ahead to my right, along the roadside, a huge green sign with a white numeral 63 emblazoned on it appeared like a friendly ghost. *This is* Tennessee *State Road* Sixty-three, *my turnoff. I hope the fog lifts as I drop off the mountain...oops, I didn't mean that literally, Father.*

To my amazement and relief, at that moment the fog began to lift and fifteen miles northwest on Sixty-three, *BC* and I dropped out of the high mountain clouds into totally clear sailing. The worry that had wrapped itself around me was gone, and I glanced up at the starry sky and thanked God for the stars shining down on me that would help me find the junction ahead. It was a well known back road, "Old US Highway Twenty-Seven" as the locals called it. I pulled over to the side of the road, grabbed a map and traced the familiar route with my finger. I smiled. *Not many people would take this winding snake of a road to Mother's house, but Dad loved it. Like a drunken serpent, Old US 27 follows*

the crooked clearwater streams of Scott County, Tennessee,
where Mother was born.

At the junction, I thought about how mom and dad met and as I passed through Oneida, the county seat and trade center of Scott County, I remembered stories from their youth and recalled how they had seen each other for the first time at a baseball game where he played for a Kentucky team. I could actually see a reflection of my mother's face as through the years she told us about how they met. Each time she would break into singing: "Take Me Out to the Ball Game" her face reflecting her memories of that time. I felt proud to be a Cooper and a feeling of courage welled up in me. "I can face my kinfolks. Mother is the key," I told BC as I patted his dashboard and continued, "though I was the middle of five boys, and the one who broke mother's heart more than the other boys, I feel like her favorite son."

That statement seemed to dispel the fear that my "vacation" would become a crash course on rejection.

BC and I sped along in the night as the black road slithered over and around knobs and ridges northward and crept across the Kentucky state line into McCreary County, Dad's birthplace.

Eight miles into the Bluegrass State, when I turned off Old 27 onto East Apple Tree Road where Mother lived, my heart shifted into high gear, and I jerked a look up the hill toward her red brick house. The lights of home were burning brightly! I lit up as I turned onto the gravel driveway. My spirits soared, and I shouted to the familiar poplar trees that welcomed me, "Mother still loves me; she's waiting up for me. *Oh God, please forgive me for breaking her heart and ruining her life. Please make this a good visit."*

When I opened the car door and stepped out, the familiar call of whip-poor-wills balanced the cacophony of katydids in the trees and told me I had been stupid to worry and everything would be okay.

Things soon became better than okay. With her arms wide open, Mother appeared in the doorway. Her radiant face chased away my dark worries, and when she embraced me, her warm arms squeezed out the anxiety that had racked my body and tormented my mind. The prodigal son had returned home at midnight. Despite the late hour, several hours past mother's bedtime, we had a fantastic time together before we retired for the "night."

I slept like I'd gone to heaven, and at daybreak, woke up to the earthly aroma of frying bacon. *I'm home. Mother's in the kitchen. I've slept through the night without a flashback to prison or a nightmare about hell.*

Thanks to a habit formed in prison, I bounced out of bed and said to my maker, "Good morning Lord, I love you. What are you up to today? I want to be a part of it." Having thus committed my day to God, I dropped to my knees, straightened my body into a prone position and pushed my weight up on all fours to do my usual routine of one hundred consecutive pushups followed by the same number of leg raises.

Minutes later when the exercise session was completed, I was breathing hard but felt strong and joyful, with all the juices flowing. Once again, I thanked God for the day and headed for the bathroom that smelled of Ivory Soap. I gargled Listerine, another of mother's old standbys, washed my face with Ivory and looked into the mirror. My reflection told me a special kind of new day had dawned. I smiled and said out loud, "The old bank robber is dead and will never hurt anyone again."

At the breakfast table, however, a voracious appetite took control and I hurt myself by stuffing in too much of mom's country fixings. I ate two eggs, sunny side up, three pieces of farm thick bacon, a big glob of sweet fried apples and three biscuits, washed down with dark black coffee. Eating so much shocked me. Prison's tasteless food had taught me to eat just enough to fuel my body. I told Mother I felt like a teenager with a bottomless pit for a stomach.

She was pleased. Her beaming face made me feel good, too. Despite my stuffed stomach, I felt relaxed; the old tensions and mistrust, gone. We were caught up and talked about happy times, good times, rather than the hurt I had caused the family. Listening to her, I realized she hadn't changed a bit. She was the same Christian woman I avoided during my bedeviled days, but I had changed tremendously as reflected by how much I enjoyed her company. Now, as if through new eyes, I saw her in a totally different light. She was not only my loving parent; she was my sweet sister in Christ, and her love and fellowship were family treasures to be possessed.

After breakfast my new "girlfriend" and I washed and dried the dishes. And then held hands as we took a walk. On the back porch we passed an old wringer type washing machine. "Is this the same wringer that ate my six-year-old thumb for lunch?" I asked.

"The very same one...but you were five."

I looked at my thumb and laughed. "You have a modern type in the laundry room," I said, questioning mother as to why she would have two machines.

"I keep it for looks; it takes me back to many good memories...when you boys were growing up."

"I'm glad, mom; but it reminds me how much better you have it now."

"Remember when many of the women at Camp Number Six went down to the creek and beat the family clothes on the rocks, to wash them."

"I remember that West Virginia coal camp and you beating me down at the creek with a willow switch."

Mother laughed.

"I'm glad you kept the washing machine...and glad you threw the willow switches away."

"I'm just thankful you didn't use the washing machine wringer to punish me."

I laughed to myself. *Thomas Wolfe was wrong. You can go home again. I've never been so much at home in my life.*

10

An unforgettable family moment came after lunch as we stacked the clean plates on the counter and sat at the kitchen table. It was August 23rd. We shared the morning devotional from Robert Schuller's Daily Power Thoughts, the devotional guide of my faithful friend who helped me make it through prison. The lesson of the day was titled, God Power Within and the scripture lesson was taken from John 12:32 in the New International Version.

"When I am lifted up from the cross, I will draw everyone to me."

I wept.

Mother leaned over toward me and asked what was wrong.

I knelt at her feet. "Mama, all those years in darkness, I made fun of the cross and ridiculed the blood of Jesus Christ."

Mom placed her hand on my shoulder and wept with me.

In between sobs, I moaned, "God has forgiven me. Can you find it in your heart to forgive me, too?"

She wiped her tears with a corner of her apron, took me by the hand and raised me up to stand before her. My body tingled as mom stretched on tiptoes to her full height of five-feet to embrace me.

In her arms I melted but she sounded like a Sunday school teacher when whispered in my ear, "Ken, the cross was God's will for our Lord, Jesus Christ, so that we could be redeemed through his blood."

I shuttered at the thought of blood and *saw* Eli die in my arms at the chow hall in the Rock.

Mother pulled back and eyed me with a worried look. She said, "Yes, that is a serious matter, but I forgave you for that a long time ago, but I need to ask your forgiveness for something."

Stunned by the flashback to Eli's death and her words, I plopped into the chair behind me.

Mother stroked my hair like I was still her tow headed child. "When I visited you in prison, I could see a change in you, son, but I couldn't believe you had really changed."

Tears filled my eyes, but an aura of peace descended upon me as she continued, "Now, I know you are a changed man through Christ. I'm so glad....I won't worry about your salvation anymore."

I felt high, higher than a high from the most powerful surge of adrenaline from robbing banks. I blurted, "This quiet high is better, sweeter..."

Mother interrupted me. "The Bible calls it peace that passes understanding, my dear boy."

Before I could react she sang a line from a song she had sung to me when she visited me in prison, "Peace, peace, wonderful peace flowing down from the Father above."

I rose up and hugged mom. "I wish June could be here with us; I miss her so much."

With the tips of her fingers mom touched the gold ring on my finger. "June is another reason I think you'll stay out of trouble...make it out here, and not go back to prison."

"You mean because she'd kill me!"

With a twinkle in her eye, she said, "For sure, but I'm thankful God gave you a wife who is a strong Christian, an independent woman who loves the Lord and you enough to talk truth to both of you."

"June really does that," I said, laughing. "What a blessing she is; She talks to God all the time and I have peace of mind knowing she puts God first and worships Him rather than me."

Mother nodded. "She is a woman of God and that's the reason you have peace, peace, wonderful peace flowing down from the Father above."

Mom's energy at 69 amazed me, but I said, "Even *Wonderful Peace* sings so much better out here than in the joint."

She didn't know what to say at first but then resorted to humor, saying, "Being at peace doesn't mean you can't still be a nut."

I laughed and said, "Let's sing about peace some more."

To my surprise, rather than singing another verse of *Wonderful Peace*, mother belted out, "Amazing grace how sweet the sound that saved a wretch like me; I once was lost but now I'm found, was blind but now I see."

I dabbed tears, held my hand up to acknowledge I was a wretch and joined her as she sang the same verse again. This time we both raised a hand on the "wretch part" laughed like two little children in Sunday school and did a "high five." Mom said, "You remember that Amazing Grace was Daddy's favorite song?"

I nodded and leaned back in my chair. "When I was a wee lad I sang it with him as we traveled to churches to preach," I said.

"Maybe those trips were a glimpse of God's will for your life."

"What do you mean?"

"All those scripture verses you memorized with him, all those sermons you heard; perhaps you will go out and preach them some day."

Goose bumps rose up on my arms and a chill settled over me. "I don't know about all that; Mother, I feel unworthy to call myself a Christian much less a preacher someday."

"Remember the message you received as a kid of ten?"

"Sure, I remember it well. I was playing under the oak tree outside the front yard, all alone, when a voice spoke to me in my heart, 'When you grow up you'll be a preacher like your Grandpa King,'"

Tears filled mom's eyes, and I was suddenly uncomfortable. *Is it because mother is talking about preaching?* To escape, I turned to her and said, "While you clean up the kitchen, this preacher creature from the Florida swamp' will use up some of his animal energy on the basketball court."

"Listen, Florida Gator, you'd better not whup up on any Kentucky Wildcats. You hear me!"

I loved mom's keen sense of humor and her love for sports. A smile lit up my face all the way to the car. Buckling up the seat belt, I mused, *June and mother have a lot in common besides me. With all their hearts, they both love God, me and sports. No wonder a sports nut like me has finally found peace of mind.*

My peace of mind didn't last long as I drove on the main highway to the basketball court in Stearns. About a mile from mother's home in Revelo, all tranquility was snatched away when a flashing blue light appeared in the rear view mirror. Unable to believe what I was seeing, I blinked, swallowed hard and felt blood leave my stomach and rush into my chest. My heart pounded like a jack hammer and the hair on the back of my neck became electric. *It's a cop; they have come for me, to arrest me, ship me back to the pen in Florida...*

My body slumped, but to control myself, I gripped the steering wheel. That seemed to help and eventually fear began to give way to reason. *There are no cuffs on your wrists, Coop; settle down. It's Moe's zany prophecy: "the police will send an officer to welcome you."*

A mixture of mirth and fear burst out of me like a volcano erupting, but I covered my mouth to stifle the explosion and pulled the car over to the side of the road. I rolled the window down and waited for the officer. *Sure hope he didn't see me laughing.* Before the patrolman stepped out of his car, I mouthed my personal version of an oft used scripture verse that was perfect for the occasion. *God has given me a spirit of power and of love and of a sound mind. I have nothing to fear.* A calm feeling came over me and in the outside mirror I watched the uniformed officer approach. *It's a local sheriff's deputy, a strapping young man in a hurry; hope..."*

"Good afternoon, sir," he said as he leaned down and peered at me through the window. "I stopped you to talk with you for a moment."

"Sir, I thank you for your courtesy, was I speeding, er...breaking the law?"

"No, you weren't."

"That's a relief, sir," I said, irritated that my voice sounded unusually high pitched and weak.

The young officer coughed. "Captain told us to pull you over and check your papers, a Travel Permit from your Florida parole officer, please." He stuck his big paw through the window.

My hand trembled as I leaned over and took the authorization papers out of the glove compartment and handed them over to him. "Here it is, sir," I said.

He studied the packet, returned it to me and said, "Cooper, you're the guy alright ... appears everything is in order, visiting your mother on East Apple Tree Road, I see, but I do have one question, how in the world did you get out of prison in three years on ninety-nine?"

Dumbfounded, I felt the blood leave my face, but then I remembered Moe's song and his warning to look out for the police because they would be looking out for me. I took a deep breath and asked, "Before I answer you, sir, do you mind if I ask you a question?"

"No, I guess not."

"Do you believe in God and miracles?"

He looked at me like I was crazy, "What in the world does that have to do with it?"

"If you don't believe in God and miracles, you wouldn't believe me."

"Er, I think I know what you mean, so...er, I'll let you go for now, but don't forget we've got our eyes on you."

"I understand, sir, and thanks for letting me go; I'm headed for the sports complex at Stearns to shoot some hoops."

"That's my game; wish..."

He stopped in mid sentence. A grin stretched my lips and I said, "I wish you could, too; looks like you could do a three-sixty slam dunk."

He coughed and appeared taken aback. "Yes, I can, er, well, take it easy; Cooper, and hope I don't have to see you again."

I chuckled and hooted the rest of the way to the ball court. *I'm high as a kite on joy juice; glad he didn't give me a sobriety test, I would have flunked it. Thank you Lord for Moe's warning; he was right; he was right as usual. Wow, am I high; this adrenalin flow is perfect for hoops especially if that young deputy stops by. Would I ever like to see his game...would it be hoops or ooops?"*

Despite the joy juice flowing, when I approached the park where the court was located. I realized I was more than a little frazzled. I stopped at a nearby empty parking lot that sported a public pay phone and made an imaginary phone call to Moe who was still stuck in Lawtey Prison. Standing in the booth, I spoke into the phone and said, "Moe, wish you were out of prison so I could really talk to you; your dadgum prophecy is coming true about the cops."

Of course an imaginary Moe could not console me, but in my mind I could hear him laughing too loudly and saying, "How do you like my song, now, ole buddy?"

I felt no humor in that thought so I dropped several coins in the machine and called June at work in Florida. She was surprised to receive a call from me at work, but when I shared what had happened and expressed my anxious feelings about even playing basketball, to my chagrin, June took a light-hearted approach to the problem and summed up my state of mind in *Monopoly* terms: "Remember our game last week. It's a wonder, Coop, the officer didn't tell you to drop the dice and go straight to jail; do not pass Go and do not collect $200... my gut feeling is that you will land on your bat feet at Park Place and whup up on those kids like they wuz cops."

A feeling of confidence came over me and I said, "Okay, you're right as usual, but please get serious enough to pray for me for the next couple of days 'cause I'm not real comfortable being up here away from you."

"No, but you're the one who needs to lead us," she said. I coughed and said, "Okay; let's pray right now: Father, I thank you for taking care of us as your children and please be with me as I face some of the people who haven't forgiven me...help me know that it's going to work out all right in the end. Amen. "

"Amen," she said and then added, "Ken it goes both ways; thanks for being there for me when I need you...you're my security blanket whether you say or pray things that make me feel better or not."

"What's a husband for, my dear wife?"

71

FREE
By Ken Cooper

"Hey, you Florida Gator, just remember to pray for the poor Kentucky Cats before you whup up on them at Park Place."

11

I looked around "Park Place," a modern recreation complex built a little more than a "three-point shot" from McCreary County High School, my old school where as a junior I played basketball. *Amazing that little brother Paul started while I warmed the bench.* I took a deep breath and thanked God for the moment. *Thank you, God, for a homecoming day in paradise. Wish Paul were here, wow!* It looked like heaven to me. Everywhere I looked, I saw green: trees, grass, basketball and tennis courts, and a little league ball field: a virtual garden full of people having fun.

My homecoming turned out to be fun for me. I was comfortable and relaxed, but ready. The young locals were warming up to play my favorite game, Three-on-three Half Court. The first team to score ten baskets would win the contest. Still high that the police officer had let me go, I felt free, alive, ready for action and my warm-up shots showed it. Despite making most of my attempts, when sides were chosen by two youngsters about the age of my oldest grandson, it shocked me that a kid would choose an unknown fifty year old at all. The team leader who pointed at me to let me know he had picked me to play on his squad, did not make eye contact and that was a red flag, but I felt relieved he chose me.

One player was left out. A red faced teen they didn't choose hung his head and sat down on a park bench to watch. *He must have no game at all.*

I stretched to warm up some more, grabbed a ball and dribbled in circles. In between bouncing the ball I introduced myself to my team mates, Randy and John. I told them I was glad we were not running full court. They laughed as if they caught my drift, but their eyes and body language told me they didn't think I could do much running, period. Worse yet, their downcast faces told me they didn't expect to win with me on their team. I could understand their doubts. The youth I would guard appeared to be less than half my age and showed quick feet and a good eye shooting the ball during the warm-up.

Motivated to prove my young teammates wrong, in between shots, I studied the player I would defend. The way he carried himself and his appearance gave him a vaguely familiar look. I smiled. *Betcha I beat his father in the high school gym over there at McCreary High.*

From that point on, I felt loose and able to concentrate on how to defend his moves and shots. When the game started, I held my own and when my team had the ball I performed well on offense. To his amazement, I outscored him. He didn't know for the past three years I had competed with some of the best basketball players in America... in the Florida prisons. And to his chagrin, my team won two out of three games. I loved the fact that he and the other Kentucky youths were shocked that an "old man" they called, *Sir,* could play at their level... on their home court. Really, I was amazed and thanked God for being with me and allowing me to play in a fun filled zone.

With the rubber match and championship victory secured, to acknowledge the Lord as *Number One in* my life,

I pointed one finger toward heaven, turned, shook their hands and left the court "on top of the world."

Strolling off the concrete pad onto a red clay path, I felt as free as the puffy white clouds chasing the sun across the sky. Two hours of playing hoops had left me dehydrated, so I stopped at a concession stand midway between the hoops court and a little league ball field down the hill. I grabbed a Gatorade, gulped it down and headed for the miniature ball park. In my ecstasy, I didn't sense that a dark tempest hovered over me and would threaten my freedom.

Oblivious to what was about to happen, I stood behind the backstop and watched preschool children play T-ball. I loved it. A tiny youngster in a uniform two sizes too huge knocked a baseball off a giant peg, scampered to the wrong base or ran into his mother's arms...in the stands. I laughed with the crowd and felt a part of them. Prison had robbed me of a sense of belonging in groups of people outside the fences that had separated me from them for almost four years. And in lockup I really missed mixing with families, especially young parents with kids. As I laughed, for the first time that day I felt okay about myself and okay about being free. In that moment out of time a peace like I felt at mom's settled over me. And somehow I felt loved.

But the positive feelings were short lived. The second line of the second verse of Moe's song was about to be sung.

Out of the corner of my eye I saw a man scrambling from the bleachers. He rushed toward me, his face blood red as he stormed me like a raging bull. He raised his fist and blasted me, "What are *you* doing here?"

I was taken aback. A supercharge of adrenaline coursed through my body; my muscles tightened, my mouth dropped open, but no words came out.

His contorted face and clinched fists told me he was dangerous like the enraged convicts I had avoided. The shot of protective juice kicked into a higher gear and energized my brain as he screamed a second time. "I asked *you* a question! What are *you* doing *here*?"

My body was on high alert, my face turned from pale pink to crimson. My right arm twitched, but somehow I managed to not lose control, stepped back and studied his enraged eyes. When words finally came, I stammered, "I-I-I'm watching kids play T-ball."

"Oh no, you're not!" he shouted, jerking a long finger toward the parking lot. "You're outta here, mister!"

Anger mixed with indignation pumped a third charge of adrenaline into my blood stream; the hair on my neck stood up, but again I held my composure. My brain knew why if my body didn't. I was on ninety-nine year parole, determined to not be violated and shipped back to prison. It would take just one lapse, one mistake and I'd go back to prison for life. I bowed my head, humbled myself, threw up my hands in what must have looked like surrender and muttered, "Why?"

"You're Cooper aren't you?" he bellowed, growing louder with each word.

"Yes, I am," I whispered. That's when I figured... like the small town cop, he recognized me as the Cooper recently released from prison.

I'd better get out of here before he does something really crazy.

Like a scolded child banned from the family room and forced to his bedroom by an angry parent, I inched past him toward my car.

The little boy within me was raging so it shocked me that I was leaving, but it shocked me even more to hear the words that unexpectedly came out of my mouth when I turned back to him and said, "I'm going, but I expect to see you in a church pew tomorrow." He appeared as shocked as I was.

As I drove away I replayed the look of astonishment on his face and laughed about the strange words I'd spouted, "...see you in a church pew tomorrow." Then it hit me that this was part of Moe's warning, "Even the people in the church pews will not forgive you."

"Lord, did you do that? Did you foresee this incident, put those words in Moe's mouth and then in mine?" I mumbled out loud. It occurred to me that talking to God about my frustration might help rid my body of rage. I commiserated with God and to myself, *He must have had small children in that game. When I closed the car door and slipped on the safety belt,* I shook my head in disbelief. *He didn't want me to watch his kids play T-ball. Incredible! He's certainly not a Christian I'll see in a church pew tomorrow.*

On the way home the words *see you in a church pew tomorrow* played over and over in my befuddled brain. I stopped at a pay telephone booth to place a collect call to June so she could talk and pray with me, but she didn't answer the phone. *Wish June or Moe were available....wonder what his take would be? Would he believe that the red-faced young man could be a Christian who attended church? How preposterous an idea...even for Moe!*

When I turned into Mother's driveway, I told the Lord that I dreaded going to church with my mom the next morning, but He didn't say anything to me.

That evening, since the Lord ignored my cry for help, I called June and talked out my feelings. Rather than battering her with a blow by blow account, I told her, "Today in the space of two hours two of Moe's prophecies that I would be rejected came true."

"What are you talking about, Ninety-Nine?" She asked with a higher pitch to her voice than usual.

"The ones about the police and the street people."

"You mean his warnings that society would reject you?"

"Yes, exactly, remember the words...no, I'll sing it to you.. *The po-leece and the judges, the bankers, street folks, church members in the pews are mumbling and grumbling,, 'Where is the justice? There's terrrrrible, bad news....'*

She interrupted me: "So two of the groups of people grumbling about your getting out of prison have stepped forward and shouted... 'You're not welcome in our town, Mr. Bank Robber!'"

"That's about the size of it..."

June's sense of humor kicked in. "That means you still have the judges, bankers and people in the church pews to look forward to."

"I can hardly wait."

"I was teasing you, sweetheart; sounds like you're having a hard time with this."

"I am; I guess I'd better get ready to be rejected by some of the people...from now on."

"Ken, could it be that it bothers you that you've been out of prison for a year and it's still happening?"

"Yeah, I did my time....maybe not enough for my crimes, but I want the whole thing to just go away."

June spoke the truth as a loving uncondemning parent would. "You'll be known as a bank robber the rest of your life, Coop."

"Yes, I know...and can accept it in my head... but not in my heart..."

June said, "We should be thankful you aren't stigmatized by other crimes that people hate a lot more than bank robberies."

I thought of sex offenders and murderers and said, "How right you are. Thanks, honey; I needed that, but keep on praying for me, especially tomorrow when I go to church and face the people in the church pews."

"Speaking of church, why don't you lead us in prayer, and be sure to ask God to give us both a good night's sleep...I miss you so much!"

"Okay, here it comes: *Father, you have taught us to thank you for all things so I thank you for the police officer and young man at the ball park letting me know that I'm a marked man...uh, well you know what I mean, Lord...please help me to trust you enough to believe you really will help me accept the hatred and rejection of people...'cause you know I sure do deserve it. And please give us a good rest tonight. In the name of Jesus, Amen!*"

79

"Amen! I love you, but that wasn't your best prayer, Ken."

"This is one time I wish you led in prayer...I really didn't feel like praying."

My wife and big sister in Christ ignored my self pity and said, "Call me tomorrow afternoon and let me know how it goes."

"I will! Good night, June, I love you, too; miss you; need you; wan...."

"Enough of that" she interrupted, "You keep that up and I'll be on the next plane."

"Honey, I'm headed for the airport in Knoxville right now."

"Good night, silly!"

"Good night!"

12

In my nightmares, angry-eyed cops with guns blazing and red-faced young men swinging baseball bats chased me. I couldn't outrun them and the only place I could hide was in a prison that resembled *the Rock* but had fences that appeared to be thirty feet high and ten feet thick. Like a terrified bank robber on the lam, I was stuck between the mob chasing me and the prison. I couldn't go forward and I couldn't go backward, so I tossed and turned the horrible night through.

When morning sun rays burst through the cracks in the venetian blinds and woke me up, I came out of the nightmare and realized my body was soaked with sweat. *Thank God; it's a nightmare; I'm okay. I'm... at Mom's house. Thank you, Lord. Whew, what a horrendous nightmare.* A feeling of great relief flooded me as I realized I was not running from the law or headed back to lockup. I thanked God for my freedom...for being in Mom's house instead of waking up in prison one more morning. I eased out of the bed. When my feet hit the floor, I voiced my usual greeting: "Good morning, Lord; I love you. What are you up to today...I want to be a part of it" and added, "I'm glad it was only a terrifying nightmare."

As I staggered to the bathroom, I continued to thank God that my nightmares were not real. *I'm free; I'm free and flowing... like this cold water on my face.* But after a hot shower, when I slipped on my Sunday go-to-meeting best I felt like I was in a straightjacket. I frowned at my face in the mirror. Out loud, I moaned, "Coop, you should feel like a million dollars; you're decked out in a gorgeous blue blazer...brand new gray trousers, a red and blue paisley tie over this white shirt... but it feels like a prison uniform."

Mother stuck her head around the corner and interrupted my thoughts.

"Talking to yourself, huh; you look absolutely stunning. How I wish your dad and grandpa could see you now. I'm so proud of you, Ken."

"Don't blow smoke, mom! You'll have to confess that fib as a sin."

"I'll meet you at the altar," she said with a grin as she took my hand and guided me into the kitchen for breakfast.

Two cups of coffee washed down two eggs with fat back bacon and biscuits into my nervous stomach. Then, two miles and five minutes later when mother and I arrived at First Hickory Grove Baptist Church, the old home church of the family, I feared I would throw up. The little white frame building loomed before me like a giant bill board with black capital letters scrawled on it: THIEF....THIEF...THIEF. At that imaginary sight, I staggered and my breath left my lungs. But I couldn't expel my guilt and shame. My conscience spoke to me; *I stole from the offering plate as it was passed around. THIEF IS RIGHT, Oh my God, please forgive me!*

Mother glanced at me and placed her hand on my arm as we ascended the concrete steps leading to the front door. I wanted to die. *As a teen I made fun of the cross and ridiculed the blood of Christ.* When my hand felt the cold steel of the door latch, my body shuttered and I paused. Mother grabbed my other hand and led me inside. There, facing the front of the sanctuary, I could *hear* my Grandfather King preaching, "Repent of your sins and be born again. Come to this mourners' bench and Jesus will wash you white as snow with his blood." The great, yet humble man of God had been dead for twenty years, but his sermon played anew in my soul as glimpses of Grandpa preaching flared up to haunt me.

As we stepped forward into the foyer, mom squeezed my hand and asked me if I were okay. I dropped my head, lied and said I was, but felt better when the door closed behind us. I looked up. Grandfather was not standing at the altar preaching, and the heady aroma of pine wood filled my nostrils and carried me back to a happier childhood. I gazed at the pulpit and focused on a bench where Grandpa sat with other elders, "men of the cloth," and deacons.

I paused for a moment and thanked God for my grandfather: The Reverend George King was a beloved man of God known throughout the eastern Kentucky northern Tennessee hills as Preacher George. He couldn't read nor write, but memorized the scriptures he preached.

Then when we stepped toward the front of the sanctuary, I thought of the earlier conversation with Moe and relived the routine Grandpa and I went through when I was a towheaded kid. Before we jumped into his big black Chevrolet sedan and headed for a church somewhere in the mountains, we sat under an apple tree in his front yard. There I read scripture verses to him, time after time, until we both knew them "by heart."

I glanced down at mother's face, smiled and caught a glimpse of the truth. *It must have been a conspiracy. The Word of God found a home in my heart and refused to die. Grandpa King has been dead for two decades, but his awesome preaching and his presence surround me now.*

Making our way to Mother's pew, the third one from the front on the right, where the elderly women sat, I glanced toward the front of the church again and almost fainted. A picture of a gray casket appeared in my mind at the mourner's bench; it was my father's bier. With a deep sigh, I *revisited* his funeral service, three months after Jennie's death, the last time I'd been in the church. I relived my rage toward God when I stood at the graveside and shook my fist at Him, and told God to "go to hell."

I murmured out loud, "Oh, God, how embarrassed all the family were that day...please forgive me!"

Mother tugged at my arm. "What did you say?"

"Please outlive me."

She frowned but didn't respond. *What a stupid thing to say!* I thought. When we sat down in golden oak pews, as hard as any sinner's heart could be, I remembered the years of depravity, bowed my head and continued to repent. Grief for my sins filled my heart and spilt out of my eyes. I seemed to lose my equilibrium and hoped I wasn't mumbling out loud. I asked God to forgive me for stealing from the church, from banks, for going my way and falling deeper and deeper into darkness. Oblivious to those around me and to the fact that I was sitting on the women's side of the building –something men didn't do - I asked God to forgive me for hurting dear sweet Mother, my daughter, the women hostages, the family and ruining the Cooper name. I had asked forgiveness a thousand times, but this time it was so real torrents of tears flowed down my face.

To regain my composure, I blew my nose, wiped my eyes and gazed through a side window, hoping Mother, and others making their way in and sitting down had not seen me weeping or realized my pitiful condition. But once more my mind wandered and swept me across the church yard, down the hill to a cemetery...a glimpse of pall bearers as they carried Dad's cold body and buried it beneath Grandpa King's grave site, next to my brother, Ted. Grief overcame me again and I wanted to die. Thankfully, mother and those around us seemed unaware of what was going on with me.

Thankfully in that moment, Leonard Godsy, the Sunday School superintendent, rescued me when he stood up and announced it was time for us to go to our assigned classes. To say I was reluctant to attend the men's Sunday school class was a gross understatement. I would have to face accusers, friends of my family, who would condemn me for my crimes with their cold eyes if not with their harsh words. But when I passed through the door into the room where the class met, the only thing I saw were two vacant chairs in a circle of a dozen men. I eased over to the seat closest to the door and sat down. When I raised my head, my body tingled. All eyes were on me. I flashed back to the "spotlight" where the FBI interrogated me in the hospital following the shooting. The teacher made an attempt to rescue me. "Welcome, Kenneth; Welcome! I'm Denzil King. I taught your older Cooper brothers in school. We're glad you're here." *Wish I were,* I thought. Not knowing what to say, I acknowledged his kind words with a nod.

At that moment a man walked through the door and looked for a vacant seat. He came over to take the chair next to me. As I looked up into his face, my eyes must have bugged out. It was the young man from the T-ball field. He was red-faced and his body seemed to stiffen before he exhaled deeply and plopped onto the chair beside me.

I sat there amazed, shocked, trying my best to not grin at what God was doing, but I didn't succeed. I turned my face from his. A slight smirk widened into a crescent shaped smile that soon stretched from ear to ear. It seemed to me the Lord was a "character" of sorts and was getting his kicks out of demonstrating his power in a bizarre way. The man, who had judged, embarrassed and threatened me, was indeed in church with me and forced to sit right beside me. I loved the moment and held my hand over my mouth to keep from expressing my glee and shock. The strange words spoken to the red faced man as he forced me to leave the ball field had come true. *I'll see you in a church pew tomorrow.*

With a sneaky sideways glance I noticed that the young man's red face had turned into a scarlet frown. He was upset and uncomfortable. He fidgeted in his chair. In fact, we both fidgeted our way through the class discussion. The key memory verse was "Judge not that you be not judged." I was certain that this moment had been orchestrated by none other than the God of the Universe for two of his judgmental children.

It was amazing. My amazement turned into astonishment as the day continued. The whole experience was apparently God-directed. The timing was ingenious. The plan was perfect. It was a heavenly conspiracy.

13

The first part of the plot was addressed by my Sunday school-teacher-mother when I joined her back upstairs. "This Sunday is Communion Day, son."

In my silence, mom read my troubled mind and said, "Don't fret; it's a day when each participant in the Lord's Supper comes face to face in a special way with their sins."

An anxious grunt escaped from my gut, but I didn't say anything. Mother cleared her throat and continued,

"Each person is given an opportunity to make things right with God and their neighbor."

The red necktie mother bought me for the occasion seemed to suddenly tighten around my throat, and I could barely swallow. *This is a conspiracy. I hate "my neighbor" from the ball field.* I squirmed in the pew next to my unsuspecting mother, wondering what else God was up to.

As the Communion elements were served to the congregation I bowed my head and wept. And in my weeping I truly forgave the young man and found forgiveness for my feelings of rejection and hatred as I prayed, *Lord, please heal my victims that feel this way toward me.* In that moment I felt an internal cleansing. By the time the service ended with the traditional parting hymn, a feeling that I was united with the church came over me.

That assurance caused me to forget the conspiracy theory and an aura of euphoria continued all day as my mom and I shared lunch and visited relatives on my deceased father's side. There was not an ounce of condemnation in any of them. I felt really free and noticed that I was anxious to get back to church for the evening service.

Given the bizarre two-part drama of the morning, however, I eased onto the back row and sat with Uncle Dean, Mother's kid brother who was barely two years older than me. Just before the service began, though, the pastor came back and asked me to move up to the very front row. I looked at him like he was crazy, but then stood up. He escorted me to the privileged pew at the front of the church. My blood pressure rose and I braced for the worst. My eyes darted to the place he indicated, then to the people sitting there next to the vacant spot. I was to sit on the aisle at the end of the first pew. Beside me would be two children. Seated on the other side of them was their father... the young man from the T-ball field! My jaw dropped and I hurriedly clamped it shut, took a deep breath and sat down. My pulse quickened and my knees knocked. I questioned God, *I don't know what you are up to now, Father. Where's the wisdom in this caper? You haven't forgotten Moe's prophecy about church pews...you surely don't want an ugly scene here, on the front row, in church.*

As I prayed for self control, all I could think of was Moe's prediction that I would be rejected by the people in the church pews. I asked God, *Father is this where it will happen? Is the pastor involved? I was baptized in this church as a kid; is the pastor going to ex-communicate me?*

Finally, I dismissed that wild fear and asked God to take control, but agonized that He wouldn't as scenes of brutal conflicts in prison flashed back and kicked in a super charge of adrenaline. As I had learned to do facing prison authorities, I fixed my eyes on the pastor and locked my hands between my knees to keep them from trembling, though somehow I kept one eye on the young man. The first move came from the pastor, who stood up to begin the evening service. I released my hands from the knee lock and sat upright. After the traditional introduction that reminded me of my Grandpa King, the pastor asked everyone to take off their shoes and socks. "Tonight's our biannual foot washing," he announced.

A weird unknown feeling came over me. My feet were suddenly cold and the rest of my body hot. I jerked a look across the room at mother. Her mouth formed a firm line and she nodded her head, so I took off my shoes and socks, thankful that neither sock was holey. *Holey socks for an unholy man.* I smiled at that thought, turned and looked down the pew to focus on the young man who sat with bowed head. I smiled again. His white feet were as long as the long fellows of a lanky basketball *player. He's no different than me.* I smiled at the sight and relaxed a little bit.

But the pastor carried a basin of water and placed it in front of me. My body stiffened. I was astounded. *Someone is going to wash my feet! This is not right!* A feeling of unholy embarrassment came over me and I crossed my feet: uneasy, unsure if I wanted someone to wash my feet, or if I was worthy, confused that I would even submit to a foot washing, much less wash someone else's feet.

Things got worse. The pastor looked down at the pew where I was sitting, motioned toward me with his hand, waved at the young man and instructed him to "wash Brother Kenneth's feet." Goosebumps ran the length of my body and I swallowed a lump in my throat. I hadn't told anyone about the previous day's incident. Only God knew. Now, that same young man who was forced to humble himself and sit with me in Sunday school class had been instructed to wash my feet. I was overwhelmed by the pastor's words to the youth, and the authoritative command "wash Brother Kenneth's feet" washed around and around in my inner being. I felt dizzy, but glanced at the young man's face. Before he stood, his youthful countenance became old with deep wrinkles that told me he had died a thousand deaths. I wondered what he would do. He gulped twice, clutched the edge of the church bench and raised his body to face his pastor.

Trembling he turned, stumbled toward me, and took his place in front of me. As he knelt at my feet, he wept.

I wept, too, took a deep breath and looked down at my feet. He could have washed them with the river of tears streaming down his face. My whole body trembled. It was all I could do to sit there. I wiped the tears from my eyes and peeked at his children. Their eyes were large. They began to weep. Their faces were bright with wonder, *or is it fear?* as they watched their father mourning, tenderly holding my feet and pouring water over them.

The warm water-- his warm hands scooping the soothing liquid on my cold feet helped me calm down and brought a feeling of warmth I had never felt before. It seemed that he was washing much more than my feet. He was washing away the hatred, the hurt, and pain... rejection out of me...out of my spirit. He was doing something for me I couldn't do for myself.

When he finished he stood and returned, barefooted, to his seat, snuffing, wiping tears. The pastor motioned to me and said, "Wash Brother Larry's feet." Now, it was my turn. *His name is Larry.*

I eased by the children, slumped to my knees in front of him, lifted and placed Larry's feet, one foot at a time in the warm water. I could have washed his feet with my tears and through the blur I caught a glimpse of God. A deep love and compassion I had never experienced welled up in me and consumed me in that precious moment. Shaken to the core my hands trembled, and what seemed like an eternity later, when I finished washing his feet, I dried them with a huge white towel.

As I stood up, to my surprise, he arose and faced me. His countenance beamed. We lunged into each other's arms. It was a brotherly bear hug I'll never forget. Runny noses and tears wet our shoulders as we held each other, our bodies shaking under the power of God. We didn't care if we were making a mess. We were clean through and through and forgiven.

After church Uncle Dean introduced us. "Ken Cooper, this is Larry Watters, son of John and Flora Watters."

The young man grinned and said, "Seems like we met at the altar."

I guffawed. "Larry...*Wat...ters*," I said, in between gasps for air. And then repeated his name with an emphasis on *Watters, a* family name that fit the foot-washing moment perfectly. He chuckled. I was glad and felt restored.

14

That evening, like a big-footed teen carried away with the happenings of the day, though the temperature outside mother's house was a comfortable sixty degrees, I asked her if we could build a fire in the fireplace. "Of course, Kenny, the glow of a fire brings back the good times."

Toasting my long fellers before the yellow flames that turned blue before escaping up the chimney, I mused, "What a day, Mom! What a warm buzz! I will never forget it; thanks for insisting that I go to church with you this morning when I was dragging my feet."

Mother nodded her agreement. "I believe it's the Lord's will for you and Larry to become ministers of the gospel."

Mom was at it again so I didn't tell her I hoped to go back into prison to preach when the Lord gave me a sermon. Instead, I said, "I felt God's calling as a kid, but that was a long time ago. Too much has ..."

She interrupted me: "It seems to me Jesus has released you from prison early for a purpose and given you the perfect help mate for the ministry in June."

"There's no doubt about that on both counts. She loves the Lord more than me and has told me so."

Mom looked at me with a question in her eyes. I looked away.

"Let's pray about it right now," she said.

"Would you pray, then, mom?"

She told me "yes" with her eyes, knelt on her knees on the giant rug in front of the gray natural stone fireplace. Like her father, Preacher George King, a man of discretion and few words, mother prayed a brief, powerful prayer that eased some of the pressure I was feeling. "Dear heavenly Father, Ken and I thank you for this day and look forward to how you are going to use us in your kingdom each and every day throughout our lives. And bless June and my other sons and their families tonight, Father. Amen!"

As I said, "Amen," mother rose up like a youth, stretched a bit, sighed, sat back down, rocked a few times and nodded off. I smiled. The moment was perfect for reflection. With a reverie I hadn't felt for years I relived the first several months out of prison. Gazing into the fire, in the blue flames that burned red and ascended like yellow plumes into the chimney, I was carried back to a Florida sunset when I proposed to June.

I called June, told her about the proposal flashback, asked her to marry me again and shared about the foot washing with Larry Watters. "Honey, God did something today that changed everything!"

"Including you, I hope!" she said.

"Especially me; He showed me that he's in control of everything... even my hardheadedness, even the rejection."

"You sound like you're on a cloud; what happened?"

"I am!"

"What happened?"

"The Lord made a young man who couldn't stand the sight of me... didn't even want me to watch his kids play T-ball...God made him sit with me in church, and then he had to wash my feet."

There was silence on the other end, so I rattled off the whole incredible story, hardly letting her respond or ask questions.

Finally, when allowed to speak, she asked, "So do you feel that he has actually forgiven you?"

"Absolutely, his tears on my shoulders...his bear hug told me so."

"Ken, I'm so glad...glad you went up there to visit your mom, and now glad that you know that you can trust God to change everything."

"It's true honey; let's pray a prayer of thanksgiving right now before I hang up.?

"Okay."

"Father I come to you tonight with a happy heart...I'm so thankful that you really are involved in our life, changing us, especially me as I learned today that you use the rejection we ex-convicts feel to bring about change not only in our lives but in the lives of those who reject us. Lord, please heal my victims, and Lord, please give us a good night sleep tonight...may my sweet June rest in your arms. Amen!"

After echoing my amen, June whispered, "You'll sleep like a rock tonight, Ken...goodnight."

June's prediction came true. I slept soundly like a contented baby in his mother's arms. And after another fabulous breakfast, with a double bladed axe, I chopped and split enough fireplace wood for a month. Then, at mother's instructions, I shaved and showered before taking her to lunch at her favorite restaurant, the first of some five stops we were going to make on what she called "my special day with my son."

As we strolled into Nell's Diner in Whitley City, about half a mile from the recreation field where I "met" Larry Watters, I held Mother's arm in mine. I hadn't felt so good since my first morning with June after our marriage. It was a grand moment. To be in her company was absolutely delightful. In her golden years mom had become childlike and was sunshine afoot. I thought, *she's like my little prison buddy, Nathaniel. She loves everybody and enjoys everything, especially singing.*

A song was on her lips when a young, bright-eyed woman greeted us with menus in hand. She wanted to seat us, but Mother had another plan and wasn't shy about it. Bubbling, she touched the hostess' hand and asked, "Gretchen, may I sing a song for you?"

My sweet little mom seemed unaware of the heads turning from tables and booths. I was certainly aware. God's intervention the day before gave me confidence, but still my plan was to maintain a low profile and not draw attention. In response to mother's request, the gracious hostess gripped the menus and stammered in her best soprano, "Of course!" Her smile didn't match Mother's.

Mom belted out her song as if she was making a curtain call for a rambunctious, appreciative audience. "Peace, peace, wonderful peace, coming down from the Father above, sweep over my spirit with billows of love..."

She finished, but that wasn't all. Before the hostess could even acknowledge her, or I could intervene, Mother began again. "Peace, peace, wonderful peace..."

People stopped eating. Their faces beamed, and with forks held at half-mast and their eyes at attention, they listened.

I worried when I realized that my face felt hot, and hoped it was joy lighting my countenance, not embarrassment, or worse yet, fear. I was truly glad when Gretchen escorted us to our table, and definitely relieved when she seated us in a distant corner.

The feeling of relief was short lived, however. I noticed as I sat down, that just beyond my right elbow sat two disgruntled appearing women customers, a storm cloud of disdain hovering over them. The face right around the corner from my elbow seemed to be an apparition of Cinderella's ugliest sister. I took another look...two angry eyes penetrated mine. I strained to focus and then I recognized who she was. *It's my mother's sister... dreaded Aunt Janice!!*

She diverted her eyes and stared past my nose toward mom. Her mouth opened into a thin line that formed a sneer. Venom spewed through her lips as she hissed, "You've done it, Irene; you've totally embarrassed your family *again!*" Her eyes blazed. "And, you've ruined our meal!"

With that she stood up, yanked her purse out of the booth and said to her sister who sat beside her, "Come on Dolores!" She spat as she huffed her way toward the door.

Mother's peaceful smile followed their backs, and too loudly she said, "Thank you!" There was no malice in her voice, but the two sisters grunted, did an about-face, stood frozen for a moment with hands on hips, spun around, and strutted out like two soldiers marching off to war.

The situation amused me and during a fabulous meal, an aura settled over us that reminded me that Mother's name, *Irene,* means *peace.*

As we waltzed out of the restaurant, a feeling of sadness came over me though when I realized my visit would soon come to a close...that afternoon. *I'm worried about Mother living alone without anyone to take care of her.*

Mom seemed to read my mind. As I opened the car door for her, she turned, smiled and said, "You can open this door for me like a gentleman, but, Kenneth, I'm perfectly capable of fending for myself... I have a lot of help, too."

"You're right; I am concerned about your living out of town alone; you don't even have a car to get around," I said peaking down at her before I closed the door.

When I took my place behind the steering wheel and fastened my seat belt, I glanced over at mother. Her eyes twinkled. "Ken, I haven't driven in years. Besides, I don't need a car."

"I think you do for groceries, the bank, church; it would sure be better."

"I'm happy just the way things are, hound dog; you're barking up the wrong tree."

"It's just that this old *hound dog* loves you, Mother."

"I love you, too, Ken, but all my needs are met. One of the main things is that John picks me up once a week and takes me to his grocery store."

Dumbfounded, I focused on the road, glad that our next stop was home and then the bank.

Back home, as I opened the door for her to get out of the car, mom glanced at me and said, "The look on your face tells me you don't believe me, but you'll see before this day is over I have no trouble taking care of myself."

15

On the way to the bank at Pine Knot, the little berg two miles south of Revelo, where my father was born, mom bragged about the friendliness of the bank employees and told me she wanted to make a donation to my new *Adam* ministry.

Tears welled up, but I objected. "Mother, June and I have not taken in our first Adam yet... a fellow named Steve is coming out of prison to us but we don't' know when."

To interrupt me, she placed her hand on my arm and said, "Well then I'll be the first to donate to your new ministry."

Tears of joy overwhelmed me and I wanted to tell mother that the Adam Ministry was a vision that might not even happen, but I remained silent.

So mother continued, "I'm so proud that you will help men as they come out of prison; I'm taking you to the bank, like it or not." I wanted to talk to her about the mixture of joy and guilt boiling in my gut, but I knew there was no way I could explain it. However, when I looked at the note lying on the seat between us, I wanted to. Mother had scribbled alarming words in giant print:

Give me two $100 dollar bills.

Thank you,
Mrs. Irene King Cooper

Choking back nervous gut pains, I said, "Mother, with me beside you...for goodness sakes, please don't pass a teller that note; you'll get us both locked up."

She didn't see any truth or humor in my remark and said, "Well, that's the way I do it, and that's the way I'll do it today."

I smiled but muttered to myself that an odd new Bonnie and Clyde team was about to hit the First National Bank of Pine Knot, Kentucky. Nonetheless, I drove toward the town's only bank where I would learn a thing or two about mother's M.O.

As she stepped out of the car she said, "I'll hand them this note and they'll give me $200 out of my checking account, one for your ministry, and one for my spending money."

I didn't say a word and to my amazement soon learned Mother knew what she was talking about. When we walked into the bank, one of the officials, a young man, rose up and met us with a huge smile, called my mom, *Mother Cooper*, and asked how he could be of service. As promised, she handed him the note and before you could say "bank robbery" twice, he disappeared and returned with two crisp one hundred dollar bills in hand.

"Here you are, Mother Cooper," he announced as he presented the bills to mom. She stuffed one in her pocketbook and handed one to me.

The young banker's eyes grew large and he stared at me. Mother noticed and tried to address his unspoken fear, "This is my son, Ken; he's just up from Florida."

I thought the youth would faint. Like everyone else in the county...the police and bankers...he must have known about me and my being in town. I extended my hand; the whites of his eyes expanded and he rocked back on his heels. I wanted to laugh, but he looked terrified. His white face reminded me of young men in prison when they faced a gang of rapists. Finally he regained his balance, leaned forward and reluctantly squeezed my hand. When his cold hand touched mine, he squeaked, "Hey, I'm Oscar Slaven."

I stepped closer to him, smiled, and said, "I'm not here to do any *banking business* today."

His mouth dropped open; he jerked his hand from mine, threw both hands into the air, and chortled, "I'm really glad! I'm really glad!"

For a second, the way he surrendered to me amused me, but then a sad thought flooded my being: *Oh, God, please forgive me; this young banker's reaction to me and my flippant words robbed him of dignity and poise...please forgive me...he looked just like some of the victims during a robbery.*

I wanted to tell him about Moe's prophecy on bankers, about my change of heart, but chose to focus on mother instead. "I really appreciate your taking such good care of my mom."

He relaxed a bit and said, "Don't mention it; she's an absolute delight whether she's sings for us, or asks us for prayer requests for you and others when she visits."

I didn't know what to say, but when I gained my balance, I pulled him aside and asked, "Do you really think she's doing okay?"

Though she was across the lobby and couldn't hear us, Mother knew what I was up to and looked at me with indignant eyes.

"Yeah, Mr. Cooper, stop worrying about your mom. John, over at the grocery store, takes care of her just the same way we do."

"How's that?" I asked.

"Don't you know, he picks her up on certain days of the month, carries her to the store, helps her with shopping and takes her back home."

I was speechless. My new banker friend had washed away my worry that Mother was isolated on an island, virtually helpless and cut off from the world without wheels.

As we drove away from the bank, a spirit of joy took over and I thanked God for Mother's friends and neighbors, who were taking good care of her. *I wish Moe could have been at the bank with us.*

But my mood changed quickly as we headed east on Kentucky Ninety-Two toward my Aunt Dessie's restaurant, where we planned to enjoy dessert. To my left between the post office where Uncle Dean worked and the grammar school, where I repeated the first grade because I wouldn't obey the teacher, stood an ominous dark landmark in my early life. It was there at Mr. Brewers' old country store that I'd gotten my first taste of quick, easy money. I couldn't help smiling, however, as I relived an escapade with Jimmy Worley. How we had unknowingly toted moonshine for the store owner in Jimmy's little red wagon and offloaded it beneath a large oak tree in the woods behind the store.

"Mother, I never told you about the time Jimmy Worley and me hauled some fruit jars for Mr. Brewer; what ever happened to him, anyway?"

"Oh, he passed several years ago," she said.

"I meant Mr. Brewer, you know?"

"I know, but actually, Jimmy passed, too, in the war."

I flashed back to Eli's death in my arms and stammered, "So... so young, um...hard to believe, Viet Nam, huh?"

Mother looked at the tears in my eyes, "You liked Jimmy a lot."

"I'm sorry to hear he's gone...thought I'd look him up to see how he turned out."

"He turned out really well, son...gave his life to the Lord in a church revival somewhere up county...married, had kids, a good job."

"I'm sorry that I used to shoplift candy and stuff from Mr. Brewer with him; I wish he was still around...both of them so I could apologize."

"I didn't know you did that!" she said with a sigh.

"Yes, sad to say, I actually liked Mr. Brewer, but we did it mostly for the kicks."

Can't cry over spilled milk, but he was really good to me while your dad was in the service."

"I know. In the Navy...remember how Jimmy and I used to work around the store, getting candy and such for odd jobs we'd do for him. Well, when he decided he didn't want us hanging around anymore, we went in with the crowd during lunch time and after school and "sneaked" what we wanted."

Mother's face turned pale; unhappy with the conversation, she turned and looked at me. "Was that how the stealing started that landed you in jail?"

Warm tears blurred the road in front of me. I dabbed at my eyes, turned to Mother and said, "I'm so sorry, Mom; yes, that was the beginning of getting high on stealing, especially when we lifted things right under his nose."

Mother placed a tender hand on my arm. "Kenneth, you were always a good-hearted boy; I just can't understand it."

"It started innocently, but during the teen years when I left home to go to high school in Arizona, there was joyriding and more stealing to get my kicks."

"Ken, I'd really rather not talk about your past; that's over and done with. You're a changed man now that you're a Christian like Jimmy. You showed that last night when you washed young Watters' feet."

"You're right; I'll never forget the love and cleansing I felt. Too bad I can't stay and get acquainted... fellowship with him."

"Why don't you stay? June would understand."

"She would, but my boss wouldn't, so I'll head out as planned this afternoon."

At noon, down the street and around the corner from the grocery store we pulled into *The Spot*, Aunt Dessie Strunk's restaurant. She was my father's half-sister, but definitely a whole aunt to me. When we entered the restaurant, she rushed out of the kitchen and hugged me so tight she squeezed every bad memory up and out of my body through my ears. Well, kinda.

"Ken, you look like a million dollars," she exclaimed as she stepped back and eyed me. I jingled the money in my pocket. "I did well...used to be in the banking business."

She sneered. "Oh, get over it! Nephew, we have."

Embarrassed, I said, "I'm trying, but some folk keep reminding me I shouldn't be free."

"Listen, nephew, freedom is spelled, p-e-a-c-e."

I sighed and said, "You barefooted Kentucky hillbillies never could spell, Auntie, but tell me more about what you mean."

She cleared her throat and declared, "You've apparently made peace with God, and the law, but until you make peace with Ken, you'll never be free."

I was overcome with the truth she spoke and stood speechless.

Mother reached out, took my hand and held it in hers as she sang a line from what I called her theme song: 'Peace, peace, wonderful peace sweeps over my spirit with billows of love.'"

"Your mom is right, Ken. Peace comes through loving yourself and others."

I held my hand over my heart and said, "Okay, I promise to love me as much as I love none other than my favorite Pine Knot Kentucky aunt."

"Yeah, right, you rascal; most of your ridge-runner relatives live at Revelo and the rest of McCreary County, and they aren't in love with my apple pie."

Mother beamed and I said, "Thanks for the good word on peace, Aunt Dessie, and thanks for not condemning me for eating too much of your world's best mouth-watering homemade apple pie alamode."

Dessie ignored me, joined mom and sang another line from *Wonderful Peace* before we exchanged more love hugs and left for the home of another favorite aunt.

16

On the way to Aunt Mae's place we stopped at Maude Perkins', a long time friend of mother's. I was eager to see *Mrs. P* as we kids called her. Through the troubled teen years she had been kind to me, allowing me to dig potatoes, wash cars and do odd jobs to earn pocket money. I didn't anticipate this stop would become another lesson in forgiveness, but it did.

Mother and I were barely seated on a couch in the living room, when our host let go with her judgment of convicts. "Something has to be done with these criminals," she proclaimed, pounding a black Bible in her lap.

She had apparently just read an article about crime in a newspaper by her side. I wanted to crawl under the sofa, but Mother placed a reassuring hand on my knee.

Rather than looking at me, Mrs. P glanced up at Mother and explained, "Now, Irene, you know I'm not talking about your Kenneth, but we've got to do something about these criminals- they're robbing people everywhere, even right here in our neighborhoods...victims all over the place."

She still hadn't looked my way and Mom didn't say anything. At the word, *victims*, I wanted to die and flashed back to one in particular, who had screamed at me, "You'll never get over this...you'll pay for this the rest of your life." At that moment and even while I was doing hard prison time for my crimes I didn't know how true and prophetic her statement would be. My compulsion was to run, but I had to sit there and squirmed in the hard seat beneath me. The more I fidgeted, the higher a burning vile of anger stirred in my stomach.

Mrs. P ignored us both and continued, "We should lock 'em up and let 'em rot."

Still, Mother did not respond. She simply smiled. I felt like I'd gone to hell, astonished that Mother smiled sweetly rather than saying something...anything. I was too angry to speak but the repressed anger rose up as an indignation that drove me to defend myself and set this self-righteous old woman straight. I stared at her with scorn and judged her. *She's blind to her own shortcomings, but I can't let this volcano in me erupt and spew all over the place. "*

I wanted to keep my cool, but couldn't'. A strange kind of righteous indignation drew a sword and pierced the Bible-toting Christian. "Doesn't the Word of God teach forgiveness for all those who repent of their sins?" I asked.

"Of course it does, but we can forgive them and still keep them locked up," my adversary said, with a smile and twinkle in her eyes that shouted, "I got you!"

Mother's reaction shocked me more than our hostess' words. She got up and started for the screened door. She cleared her throat, motioned to me with a finger to her lips to not say anything more. "Thanks, Maude, I enjoyed talking to you. Drop in on me anytime."

Oddly, even in my mental state, as I walked out the door and looked back at Mrs. Perkins, I was reminded that I also had a judgmental attitude. I didn't like the feeling.

On the way to Aunt Mae's I apologized to Mother for losing my cool, but she wasn't ready to hear it. "Kenneth, you're going to have to knock that chip off your shoulder."

"What do you mean?"

"Back there, if I hadn't walked out; you would have had the last word...that's insecurity or maybe worse, you are worried about something."

"Someone, mom; she was talking about me, Mother...not the unknown prisoners, and about her fear they would steal again!"

Mother smiled and assumed the sweet but motherly tone I hated as a kid. "Do what your Aunt Dessie suggested, 'Get over it; stop worrying about the past, or the future.'"

I exhaled to dispel my anger, took a deep breath and said, "I'm sorry, Mother; you're right, maybe I do feel insecure, but I'll work on it."

"Remember what your granddaddy always told us, 'Don't worry about tomorrow; sufficient unto the day is the evil thereof!'"

"Mother, I've always fallen short of the other boys, so maybe it's not a false feeling."

A frown formed a question mark on her forehead and she said, "Well, Ken, I don't know why you would feel like you were not as good as your brothers."

"For one thing, they didn't land in prison. But even as kids, for some reason, it seemed like they were okay and I wasn't."

Mother changed the subject with humor. "Now, if you are talking about mechanical ability, you were certainly not okay," she said as she laughed and patted me on the knee.

I laughed with her. "You know how Dad was, he could fix anything, and the other brothers were much more mechanically inclined than me."

"Yes, I remember how they took their old scooters or bicycles and fixed them up."

"Mother, that's the perfect example. Because of my inability to put a bike together from parts, I made do with anything that had handlebars and pedals."

"I remember. That's when we lived at Clothier, West Virginia, but you boys all had old bikes."

"Yes, but I had the worst one, a rusted out Schwinn *girl's* bike."

Mom grinned and said, "I wondered why you rode that old bicycle."

"Well let me tell you the whole story on our way to Aunt Mae's. I rode it only at night. It was an embarrassment with its pale blue paint accented by - give me a break - pink flowers. Being a girl's bike it didn't have a crossbar and that gave me away. It was good that I was a tough kid, I didn't have to fight too many guys around the neighborhood."

Mother chuckled and seemed delighted to recall family days when I was a teenager.

I continued my tale. "Do you remember how my pals kind of tolerated being with me, and my bike they called Binky?"

"Sure, I remember. You were about fifteen at the time, tall for your age, an athlete and lady's man."

Straight faced, I said, "Yeah, that was me, good looking and chased by girls.'

110

Mother smirked and rolled her eyes, so I finished my tale. "I saw myself as a someday football star and Romeo. I rode my 'wheels' when none of my pals would see me."

"I didn't know that," Mother exclaimed and then laughed.

"Yeah, this image thing and pride problem apparently go back a long way. Sometimes I would take the old girl out early in the morning because all respectable teenage boys slept late in those lazy summer days."

"That was especially true of the Cooper boys in the sleepy little town of Clothier," mother interjected with a chuckle.

"One day, I rode Binky across the highway in front of our house and down the railroad track to see Howard Allen about summer work. He wasn't home as promised so I fast-pedaled back toward the house so none of the guys would catch me on Binky. I was flying.

When I came to the highway, I was concerned about someone seeing me. I didn't notice a car barreling down from my left until he was right there on top of me. To dash across the road in front of it, I gave a gigantic pump on the pedal. Well, I pumped so hard, and pulled on the handlebars with such force that I went flying though the air across his line of vision, handlebars still in hand, but half of the bike behind me. I landed on my face on the yellow line."

Mother laughed and then said, "I'd never heard this one; you must not have been hurt."

"I didn't' tell anyone; the impact didn't really hurt anything but my pride, but I certainly realized that something was wrong. Fortunately the car was able to stop about ten feet from me. I got up and looked back in the direction from which I'd come. There was the back half of Binky lying where I'd given that powerful pump on the pedal. I stood in my tracks for a moment and then I heard the guy in the car laughing. I snapped and threw the front half of the bicycle across the road toward the back half, and scrambled to retrieve the two pieces. The driver was still in uproarious laughter."

Mother interrupted me again. "That had to be quite a sight."

"I was so mad I couldn't see straight, but I glared at him and could have killed him with that look. But, suddenly it hit me. I was lucky to be alive. Pride had nearly killed me. I returned his laughter, walked off and carried broken Binky to the junk pile."

"So that's why I never knew what happened to Binky," she said.

I nodded and said, "I never told a soul about the incident until prison, and coming out of lockup ... seeing how people label you for life as a worthless, no good ex-convict, maybe I should have a pride problem?"

"Why did you get upset with poor Maude?"

"I was quite shocked; I believe almost anybody who really wants to change can change, and those who can, they deserve a second chance."

"It's natural for us out here to believe hard core criminals don't change."

"That's what amazing about prison, mom, probably ten percent of the guys are hardcore criminal types: sociopaths, psychopaths."

"People who have no conscience?" she asked.

"That's right; men and women who value nothing or nobody."

To change the dark subject, mother placed her hand on my arm. "Ken, I'm glad you stand up for the innocent prisoners, who should not be locked up and forgotten."

I smiled and patted her hand. I wish I'd been innocent...Ed Austin, our state attorney, says about five percent of the people in prison are innocent and another five percent, wrongfully charged and sentenced."

"Ken, speaking of charges, it bothers me to this day that you involved Howard Davidson's son, David, in that last bank robbery...how could you?"

Mother's accusation caught me off guard...I wanted to defend myself by explaining how David had begged me for months to include him in a holdup after he figured out that I was the bank robber who had struck a couple of central Florida banks, but I didn't. I sighed and said, "'I hope to visit him and ask forgiveness."

"I will pray that you can; he's such a good boy."

The implication that I was not "such a good boy" burned into my soul and sizzled like bacon in a frying pan, but I refused to give in to my emotions. I said, coldly, "I plan to do that and apologize to Mr. Davidson when I do."

"The victims...like them; it would be so good if you could... for you and for them."

I was silent.

Mom touched my arm. "Those are things I thought about...when I heard you were getting out...I was thinking of you but pray for them too."

A cloud of uneasiness hovered over me. I wanted to change the subject but couldn't. "I pray every day..well, just about every day that they will get over it...I'm just glad you prayed for me and answered my letters...most guys in there get no mail and have no one outside who cares about them."

Mother cleared her throat. "That takes us back to the truth: whether or not people can change. Thank God you've changed, and I know it. There'll be no more victims."

My mom's words called up a flood of emotions that spilled out my eyes. I pulled over to the side of the road, parked, turned to her and said, "I've been wanting to hear you say things like that, but I don't feel worthy...you've let the mother in you take over."

"You' may not be, but it's true."

"I'm overwhelmed...wish I didn't worry.""

"The Watters boy forgave you."

"Most of the people out here would not agree with him," I said as we came around a corner near Aunt Mae's.

"Most are not very forgiving, but thank God he touched Larry Watters' heart and changed his attitude toward you."

I was silent.

"There's so many victims; I'm not talking about myself...so many people hurt and they find it hard to trust the ones who hurt them again."

Tired of mom's ventilating, I wanted to change the subject but knew it wouldn't be right. My gut tightened and I said, "That's right, and it will take a long time for them to heal and for me to prove that I've really changed."

"I didn't mean you, Ken. Like I said, I can tell you're a different man than you were before prison."

"Thanks, sweet Mother, but I do mean me."

She touched my arm. "But son, you've got to move on with your life and not hold on to bitterness."

"You're right. But it's really hard to feel okay about myself with this "mark of the beast" we ex-convicts have stamped on our foreheads," I said, tapping my brow as we turned into Aunt Mae's driveway.

17

There, as expected, we had as good a visit with Aunt Mae as the stopover with Mrs. Perkins had been bad. My favorite aunt's attitude was like a ransom note from heaven. Her unconditional love set me free. She loved me, wasn't worried I would reoffend, and believed nearly everyone deserved a second chance at life, especially her nephew.

Following our reunion, I took mom home, hugged her goodbye, drove east on the Kentucky Mountain Parkway across the upper reaches of the Cumberland Mountain range headed south toward home and June on Interstate Seventy-Five. I was eager to complete my first trip away from June. *Wow, do I ever miss her...seems like my right arm is missing.*

During the first few minutes of what would be an eleven hour trip, I talked to the Lord about my reaction to Mrs. Perkins and asked him to continue to help me adjust to people's negative attitude toward ex-offenders, meaning me.

As the trees on both sides of the forest-lined highway whizzed by, I prayed a self centered prayer laced with confusion that may not have made it out of the woods: "Father, things fly by so fast out here; I need your help now even more than I did in prison. A lot of people think like negative prison guards. You are certainly giving me a crash course on how to forgive those who continue to judge me for my past sins. The Watters boy and Mrs. P... I don't like it, but if you put them in my path to teach me to forgive I'll try to do it ...'cause a lot of other folks don't...Lord, whatever it takes to help me get over the negativity of prison, Help me, Lord."

About thirty miles down the winding foothills highway that connects US 27 and Interstate 75, an irresistible urge hit me to continue on the Parkway into London and turn south on US 25 E rather than taking the more direct and faster route, I-75. "I'm not about to take that slow road, Lord," I argued and turned on to the interstate highway.

But as I zoomed down the super speedway an eerie feeling that God was displeased with me overtook me. It was almost as if a highway patrolman had caught up with me from behind and gave me a ticket for speeding. "Lord, that's amazing; You really do want me to exit and take 25-E, don't You. You're not happy; this is Your answer to my prayer?"

Just as if there had been no state trooper behind me, I pulled off the roadway, stopped and waited for a further word from God if one was forthcoming. But there was no answer from him, and I did sense a bit of peace, so I said, "Okay, I'll do it, prayer or no prayer, though it makes no sense, and it will take me hours longer to get home to June."

Of course, God didn't respond to my rebuke, and since the feeling persisted to change routes, ten miles south of London, at the intersection of U.S. 25 and U.S. 25-E in Corbin where Colonel Harland Sanders built his first Kentucky Fried Chicken, I turned off the main highway and headed southeast on 25-E that follows the trace that Daniel Boone cut through the wilderness when he crossed over the mountains at Cumberland Gap two hundred years earlier.

As Corbin grew small behind me the fifty-five mile an hour speed limit seemed like Ole Daniel Boone would pass me any moment. But as I approached Middlesboro, where I had lived two years during the bank robbing days, one of the reasons for taking that route became clear. Though I had not held up a bank in Middlesboro, tears clouded my eyes as faces of traumatized bank tellers appeared before me as reflections on the windshield. My eyes blinked to erase the look of terror on their faces. Tears poured out of my eyes but I managed to pull BC over to the side of the road to park in the emergency lane. "I'm sorry Lord; please forgive me; please heal those poor women in the banks, especially the tellers...please forgive me and heal them."

At that moment the kaleidoscope tellers' faces stopped rotating through my befuddled mind, and a feeling of overwhelming calm flooded my being. And though I didn't hear a voice, I knew God had heard my last prayer and had forgiven me. I wiped my eyes, blew my nose, laughed at myself and began to sing a song I had learned in prison through a ministry called Kairos. "Surely the presence of the Lord is in this place; I can feel his mighty power and his grace...I can feel the brush of angels' wings, there is joy upon each face...surely the presence of the Lord is in this place."

Nevertheless, as I drove toward the Gap, hackles rose on the back of my neck, so I expressed newborn negative feelings to God: "If this is you, God, and if you answered my prayer by taking me on this detour after I'd asked for help, why don't you help me get over these feelings...I sing about joy...yet I loathe myself...though I don't know how to pray,

118

I ask for your help knowing I'm not worthy of it. I deserve this overload of guilt and shame. Besides, I really don't like this weird route ...making me go out of my way...for what?"

A few minutes later when I crossed into Tennessee, I sighed, and once more talked to God about his plan, his timetable, and whatever He was about to do in my life. *"Please Lord make me alert and guide me, but please make it less eerie than the urges I felt on the highway earlier, Lord."*

About ten miles south of Cumberland Gap, the internal stirring returned and this time "told" me to turn onto a less traveled road. It took every ounce of my being to obey, but I did and turned onto a narrow side road that didn't even have a road number.

Though I was exasperated and felt foolish, I continued on the winding trail for a mile or so when to my left, I spotted an unpainted plank house perched on a hill overlooking the road. Instinctively I knew this was my destination. *This is where you're sending me, Lord?*

"Yes."

Amazed at how strong the "knowing" was, on the edge of the road carved out of the hillside beneath the home place, I parked, rolled down the window, and looked up toward the house God had led me to. *This old place has wooden shuttered windows, a screened front door, to the right, a smokehouse, and out back, two run down sheds. There's a huge white-headed man in faded bib overalls, probably seated in a rocking chair. Lord, those overalls are the same faded blue us prisoners wear,"* I said out loud and added, "What in the world are you up to, Father?"

119

18

Of course, God didn't answer me and I felt all alone and unsure of myself or of God when I stepped out of the car and stood on the road's edge. From my vantage point I could see the top of the front porch and the peak of the house, but could not see the man, which meant he could not see me. That made me nervous. *He'll send his hounds to investigate, or worse.* That thought caused me to eyeball the winding path up the hill toward the house. *I know they've got dogs, but thank God I don't see any coming yet.*

As I took the first step toward the switchback pathway worn deep by time, I noticed the name on the mail box was Jones, a family name. *The Jones name makes me feel better, Lord, but I'm scared to death.* As wary as I was, the old home place looked as peaceful as could be. To the right of the porch toward the smokehouse a little garden showcased waist high corn stalks that formed a green backdrop for huge tomatoes that hung like bright red grapes, vine ripe for the picking.

When I topped the hill, to my right strutted a gigantic Rhode Island Red rooster whose spurs appeared to be three inches long. He raised his head to check me out as he stood guard over his harem of about a dozen hens, busy pecking feed strewn on a patch of bare ground that formed the front yard. I slowed my pace and during the next ten strides, the chickens clucked and scattered to make way for me. The rooster stood his ground. Though I had been spurred by roosters I antagonized as a kid, fear did not well up in me. I was alert for his attack but more concerned about the Joneses and their dogs. *Lord, protect me from this bird; hope they're friendly people, and their dogs even friendlier!*

As I drew close enough to the house to take a peek on the front porch, a bolt of fear struck me like lightning. A huge black and tan hunting dog sat guard-dog style in front of the man in the rocking chair. *That beast looks like the mountain lion killers trained by my backwoods kinfolk.* I ran trembling finger tips over a scar on my left shoulder inflicted by a black and tan hound that attacked me when I delivered newspapers in a coal camp as a kid. The *fear* settled in my gut but ran up and down my spine.

"Hello up there," I yelped, my voiced high pitched with terror. The man waved his hand to let me know that he had heard me, but he didn't stand up or say anything to welcome me. A slight twinge of my right hand reminded me that his wave of the hand was not necessarily a friendly gesture. He could be signaling his dog to attack; after all I was intruding on the Jones' property in an out of the way area not often trespassed by strangers.

"Come on up, stranger!" the man called down to me in a friendly tone. *Thank God he's friendly!* Relieved with his neighborly welcome, in my best mountain lingo, with a nasal twang, I spouted, "Howdy; don't mind if I do."

But half way up the stairs when I reached eye level with the dog's dark wild eyes, my adrenal gland took over and shot a charge of animal juice into my blood that made me quiver all over. *I'm sure he smells my fear. This is ridiculous.* To make matters worse, as demons of terror invaded my mind, with the hair on his back bristling, the fearsome looking beast sniffed and bowed up before me. The smile that had softened my lips to greet the man gave way to a hard wrinkle beneath my nose that must have looked more like a trench line hacked out by terror. *God, help me!* When the massive monster didn't bark or growl but continued to glare at me, a painful lesson from the past blinded me: Bad dogs *don't bark...they attack!*

The man must have read my body language if not my mind. He grunted, "He won't bite you!" The beast sat down but still faced me. Even on his haunches he stood waist high. *Fearsome.*

Truly thankful the dog had obeyed his master, I laughed and yapped, "Could have fooled me!"

The man laughed and stood up to receive me. At his master's signal, the dog rolled over on his side like a playful pup and turned his back to us. I was delighted and the friendly tone of the man, the homey place helped me to relax a little bit and feel safe enough to say to myself: *Thank you, Lord, dog or no dog, I have arrived at my destination. This is not a detour; this is a divine appointment.*

My face must have looked blank and still flushed. The man tried to reassure me: "Like I told ye; he don't bite except strangers...sometimes...his name is Duke."

"Hi, Duke," I said with quavering voice as the dog stood up and eyed me again.

"Welcome, come on up and set a spell," the farmer said, as he motioned to a second rocking chair, like the first unpainted and probably homemade.

I repeated my best backwoods lingo and said, "Don't mind if I do, sir,"

"My name is Jones," he said as he placed a long yellow whittling stick he had been working on in the huge front pocket of his overalls. I guessed the golden grained wood to be a tulip poplar like my Grandpa Charlie Cooper used to whittle into a whistle for me. As Mr. Jones' sky blue eyes fastened on me I noted how closely they matched his overalls.

"Howdy; mine is Cooper," I replied as my eyes darted back to check out the guard dog. The old hound stirred, perked up one floppy ear, but plopped back down on the porch.

"There; that's a good dog, Duke," I breathed.

At the sound of my friendly voice, the dog wagged his tail. The old man's head canted a bit and he smiled as he offered his hand to greet me.

"I'm proud to meet ye, Cooper," he said and took my cold hand in his warm weathered paw. "Are ye from these parts?"

"Um...yes sir, the John Coopers from Jacksboro a long time ago," I sniffed.

"Heard of him from down the valley; is that where ye came from?"

"No, from across the state line in Kentucky...McCreary County where my clan of the Coopers settled a hundred years ago."

His eyes twinkled like Kris Kringle's and to my amazement, he said, "George Washington Cooper must be your great, great, grandpa."

My heart leapt into my throat. "How in the world did you know that?" I asked.

"There weren't many folks around back in those days so our clan intermarried with the Coopers from Wartburg, Tennessee....cousins of your line...so jest for fun we could call ourselves cousins."

I was speechless. *God, you are amazing.*

He smiled. "How'd ye happen by this way?" he asked, punctuating his question with a sideways spit of tobacco juice.

I heard the brown collection splatter on a flat rock just beyond the edge of the crude porch. Then, though I was comfortable with my new "cousin," and had just spoken to God, I couldn't believe what came out of my mouth. "God sent me." Again, my voice sounded high pitched, but strong. Hearing the words I'd spoken, I swallowed and took a deep breath.

Mr. Jones continued his whittling, looked up, eyed me, grinned, but returned to his whittling without a word. It surprised me he didn't say something or at least lift his eyebrows at my announcement. When he did speak, without raising his head, or lifting his eyes, he said, "*She's* in the kitchen; been expectin' ye."

His matter-of-fact manner and statement shocked me to the point that I froze in the moment. When I didn't say anything or move, he glanced up at me. I guess he could see that I was a bit confused and didn't know what to say or do. The corners of his eyes crinkled. With the large black-handled knife in his hand he motioned over his shoulder toward a rusty old screened door. "Go on in the house. *She's* waitin' fer ye in the kitchen."

I could feel my face flush. The hair on the back of my neck stood up. *What are you up to God? Who is "she" and what is she doing in the kitchen "waiting" for me? If God really did send me, how did the old man know it?*

I collected myself, took a deep breath and eased my way into the house. It was quaint, homey, and modestly furnished with rough colonial sofa and chairs in the living room, doilies on the furniture, family pictures on two walls. It looked and smelled like Grandma Cooper's place, but I didn't take time to really check it further. Like most Cumberland highland homes, it was spotless clean and inviting.

Into the dining room I hurried, made my way around a long family table graced by a homemade doily type tablecloth. My granny made those from flour sacks...wonderful, beautiful. Then, facing a rough oak framed doorway opening into the kitchen, I stopped when I heard what sounded like the creaky voice of an elderly woman loudly pouring her heart out to God. It was truly amazing to hear what she was praying. "And Father, I thank ye very kindly for sendin' me someone to pray with; ye know I can't share this matter with anyone but a stranger. Send me a stranger, Lord; someone to agree with me in prayer."

Gooseflesh rose on my arms and I wanted to turn around and sneak out, but amazement stopped me. I muttered out loud, "Lord, you sent me to pray with her; this is incredible," and turned my face up to whisper, "Father, this old woman hasn't seen me or heard me, but apparently she knows I'm here, or on the way. She's expecting a *stranger.* She's expecting *me.*"

I stepped into the doorway and peered around the corner. There, in a pink and blue striped gingham dress with her white hair swept back in a round grey bun, a woman knelt on a rough, white wood floor whose "sins" had been washed away by lye water. She was old... weathered, obviously the man's wife. She knelt with uplifted, gnarled hands and wrinkled brow with deep furrows plowed by a hard life. Tears filled the cracks in her face and trickled down her cheeks, but her face was radiant as she prayed, "Thank ye, Lord, for sending me a stranger."

Those words penetrated my heart. *I am that stranger; God has sent me here...incredible.* In that moment God put a love for that old woman in my heart I had never felt for anyone but June, much less for a stranger. Tears blurred my vision as I edged closer. I wanted to take her in my arms and comfort her as a prodigal son would his aged mother, but felt God had sent me for other reasons.

19

Apparently she sensed my presence, turned, dropped her hands and looked up into my face. Immediately, she leaped up like a young woman, threw her hands high and shouted, "Thank ye, Lord! Thank ye, Lord! Ye have really done it! Ye sent me a stranger to pray with!"

Rather than greeting me, she reached out, grasped my cold hand, and yanked it down toward the floor as if directing me to kneel beside her. My knees bent with hers and came down with a thud, hard against the rough floor. My first impulse was to pray for the healing of my knees, but I closed my eyes and talked to God silently while listening to her petition. "Ye knew it had to be a stranger, Lord. Ye knew I couldn't pray with just anybody about these matters."

The earnest old woman cried out to God for a long time. As the minutes dragged on, pain from aching knees overloaded my mind and made it hard for me to concentrate. After what felt like ten minutes she became still louder; pouring out her heart to God in greater desperation and passion.

She prayed as if she was actually looking up into the face of God. Water dripped from her face as she pleaded with her Father in Heaven to "heal up" the church, to stop the strife and division among its members—she spoke of things she couldn't have prayed for with a church member or neighbor. And she spoke of things that overwhelmed me:

"Lord I thank you for sending this young man; I know he has troubles too, and I pray for him. Help him love himself the way you love him and believe you about his calling.

I was amazed at her words but a groan came out of my mouth.

"But mostly, Lord, thanks for sending a stranger who doesn't know any of these people, so I can call out names...please forgive the self righteous people who think they're God, or at least they act like it."

As she named names and sins I smiled through my leg pains since I wanted her to name Mrs. Perkins for me... but my knobby knees and a feeling of guilt wouldn't let me, so I said, "Forgive Mrs. Perkins, Lord, for judging me...Lord, you know I don't deserve it..."

With that self righteous thought, the pain in my aching knees grew unbearable, but I couldn't bring myself to rise up from the unforgiving floor until she did. As the minutes passed I repented of my flippant remark about Mrs. Perkins, pushed the pain back and listened to her beg the Lord to give the church members, "especially us old biddies who try to run the fellowship" a new heart and a submitting spirit. I thought how humble and honest she was to pray for "troublesome" situations that included her as one of the "old biddies causing problems." She added, "Lord, it seems like to me that ye and the new pastor ye sent us know what's best fer this little flock. A'course ye do. So A'm askin' ye to change us, help us accept strangers like this one into our midst." Mrs. Jones hesitated. "An' Lord, would ye send us a spirit of revival right soon? I shor' am grateful, Father God."

Listening to that old woman pray reminded me of my Grandfather King. As a tow headed kid, there were times when I heard him cry out to God under the apple tree in his front yard and heard him pour out his heart to God at the wooden mourner's bench at the old church house up on the hill from his home. *The one I attended with Mother yesterday. And during the afternoon, today at Mrs. Perkins place ... "Oh, Lord, I'm such a wretch; please forgive me and wash away my hate."*

Returning from my mental detour, I sensed that God was hearing this old woman just as he had heard my granddaddy.

I yearned to be able to pray out loud like them, but without bellowing loudly. I thought about Mrs. Perkins again, how much hate I'd felt toward her. My head hung and I wept as I pleaded with God once more to forgive me. Suddenly a clean feeling came over me and I felt washed like I had been at the foot washing with the Watters boy. A smile slowly inched across my lips as I considered the moment. *I'm in the Cumberland Mountains but at the same time I'm in heaven... in the presence of God. Truly there is no time or space in the spirit world I'm now a part of. Amazing.*

Returning once more to Mrs. Jones's kitchen, I tuned into her petitions and asked God to answer her prayers. I hadn't prayed a word out loud, but a sense of peace came over me that assured me he had heard me just as surely as he heard her. *Amazing.*

When the final "amen" was said, she rose up and offered some home cooking. I checked the clock on the wall above her wood burning stove. "I hate to turn down wonderful mountain cookin, but I've got to get on the road to my wife in Florida."

She touched my hand, nodded her agreement, and led me back to the front porch, where Mr. Jones sat alone, Duke having left his master's side. I was glad about that, and despite my hurry to hit the road, without thinking about it, I stopped, looked at the kindly man and asked that he and his wife continue to pray for me, "one of his long lost cousins."

He laughed but became serious. "What would ye have us pray for?"

"My wife and I plan to start up a ministry to help men as they come out of prison. We call it *Adam*, Adopt a Man."

My host didn't say anything. He glanced at his wife with a perplexed look, so I tried to explain, "I'm telling you about the ministry God wants us to do."

"Son, we understand; we have some kin in prison...we'll pray for ye right now," he said as he knelt down on the wooden planks that formed the flooring of the porch.

His wife and I knelt, too. Once more my knees complained. *How do these old people do this? Surely I can, too.*

The mountain man called out to God and his wife prayed out loud at the same time. I focused on his petition that sounded like the brief prayer songs my grandfather prayed. He chanted in a fine melodious tenor voice, "Father, ye heard this young man's request. We thank ye kindly for helping him stay out of your way so your ministry will work. Amen."

I smiled in agreement and rose up from my knees a changed man, okay with myself and feeling a deep kinship and at home with people I'd met just minutes before. As I took a step toward the car, Mr. Jones touched my arm and told me to wait for a minute. He disappeared into the house and returned a moment later with a smile as wide as his front porch. "Here ye are my young friend; take this gift and use it to set your Adam feller free, so you can adopt him when he comes out of prison."

His words floored me and when I glanced down at the bill he placed in my hand, a crisp one hundred dollar bill, I felt weak in the knees. *It looks just like the one mother tucked away in my Bible...the one she gave me...brand new, never been spent.* My head spun with thoughts of the C-notes being ransom notes from heaven, messages from God that he had set me free from my sin debt. *Like Moe said, God's ransom note demands nothing from me.*

Mr. Jones touched my arm to bring me back to his front porch. "What's wrong, son?"

"Nothing's wrong; everything's right. I'll never forget this, sir; this is like a message to me from heaven...I can't explain it to you today, sir...someday I'll come back and tell you all about it... but today, just let me say that Satan once held me hostage to the thrill of stealing one hundred dollar bills...lots of them. I did three years in prison for bank robberies."

Mrs. Jones gasped, but Mr. Jones didn't flinch. "Well, ye sure didn't steal this one. It's a free gift...no strings attached."

"That's the whole thing, sir. Neither did my mom when she gave me a C-note earlier today for the same purpose...gifts to help our first Adam when he comes out ...you

131

both showed your trust in me to use this money to help him, our first Adam -- his given name is Steve - when he comes out."

"To God be the glory; I'm planting this greenback in good soil, the soul of that feller Steve you call your Adam, Cooper."

"Please pray for Steve, and for me, that he will make it, find true freedom and stay free."

"I will, but you need the prayers of your pastor, your shepherd who looks out for you."

I stepped back in awe. "Well, uh...uh...I don't have a pastor yet, sir."

"How long you been out of lockup?"

"It's been several months now...we're looking but I like them all too much to choose just one."

"Well, that will be my prayer for you, son, that you find the church that feeds you and supports your prison mission."

With one quick step I moved toward him and embraced him like I always wanted to embrace grandpa, Preacher George King. For the most part mountain men didn't hug or cry. "I'll never forget you folks; we'll find a church home, a pastor, and I'll let you know when your adopted man, Steve, arrives so you can pray for him."

"We'll do it," he said.

Not to be left out, Mrs. Jones hugged me and told me to come back when I could. Her warmth told me she meant every word. Although I was the stranger she had asked the Lord to send, when I walked back to my car, I felt less of a stranger to her, to her husband, to Larry who washed my feet the day before, to Mrs. Perkins and most of all, to myself and God. Driving back to the main road that would put me on I-75 headed toward home and June, I prayed, *Father, I wish she could have been here to meet my "cousins." Really, June and I need people like them, a church family to help God prepare us for our Adam. No doubt it's the will of God. The C-notes proved that.*

Back on the interstate, when I drove BC along the mountain ridges that overlook Jacksboro and Wartburg, I thought of Mr. Jones and wondered if he truly was a long lost but found cousin God had put in my life for his purposes. I laughed out loud and told the Lord that I would always trust him despite his strange ways of preparing me to receive a man coming out of prison. What I didn't know was how confusing, if not downright frustrating and strange, his ways would be.

20

The ten hour trip was anything but a hardship. I flew home on the wings of joy and approached Jacksonville with a song, "Like a bandit bird from prison bars has flown, I'll fly away" and was still high when I stepped through the door of our home where June was waiting with open arms. Following hugs and kisses, I spent hours sharing my experiences: the joy of being with mom, the young sheriff, the young banker, the young father and the foot washing, an elderly Mrs. P, and sweet old folks named Jones. I spent most of the time sharing about the foot washing, but I told her how God had used all of them and the gifts from the Joneses and mother to set me free from the guilt and self condemnation that had been holding me back. Even so, we discussed the rejection, trials, and frustration I went through, but now I was laughing rather than moaning. June said she was overjoyed that I had begun to see God uses blessings to encourage me as well as hardships and suffering to correct me in my continuing readjustment to freedom.

That's exactly what happened when I returned to work on Monday morning. *Neighbor* Editor Jill Simmons promoted me to the position of staff writer and assigned me to cover the north side of Jacksonville, where I lived.

However, the exultation was short lived. Given my atrocious typing speed, then a whopping twenty-five-words-a-minute, and limited experience as a news writer and editor, meeting my daily deadlines of two articles a day on breaking events while supervising page layout overwhelmed me. As a result, despite the recent mountaintop experiences and reassurance from God and June, I feared failure stood at the door, ready to pounce on me like a big cat. I was as low as I had been high in the mountains. To alleviate my depression and anxiety, and to give me a chance to meet the deadlines, I went to work at six in the morning and kept my nose in the computer six hours a day, seldom taking more than a fifteen-minute lunch break.

Within a matter of weeks, Miss Simmons became concerned about me and told me to get out of the building at noon and take a full hour for lunch. Immediately upon hearing her command, my blood pressure came down and I felt like a kid let out for recess. On my next lunch break, in glorious October weather, I sat on a bus stop bench in front of the newspaper building on Riverside Avenue, hoping the bus wouldn't come by until I finished eating. Before I wolfed my food down, I held the lunch in my hand, closed my eyes and thanked God for his gracious provision: "Father, I thank you for providing this ham and cheese sandwich and fruit June fixed for me; thanks for blessing June for preparing it and blessing it to my body. By the way, Lord, I'm sure glad it's not a glob of prison type peanut butter and jelly, and I'm even gladder I'm not waiting here on a prison bus."

That thought brightened my mood and while eating I gazed at an old wooden fence across the busy roadway. The cars whizzing by formed a blur of traffic in which a picture from the past appeared. I sat on a fence in Williamsburg, Kentucky, in front of Cumberland College, watching the cars go by with a young friend named Billy, a brilliant lad of

135

twelve. He called me Mr. Ken or Ken Lucky, and I called him, Billy the Kid. I was a troubled thirty-three-old addicted to robbing banks who had just begun working with the Christian college as director of publicity.

Billy interrupted my trance, "What are you afraid of, Mr. Ken?" Due to the stuff whirling around in my brain his question upset my mental balance and I almost fell off the fence. But I snickered, steadied myself enough to answer his question with a question of my own, "What do you mean?"

"What are you afraid of; what's your big fear, Ken Lucky?"

"The fear of failure because of getting caught," I said, surprised that those words came right out without thinking.

Billy laughed. "That's funny; I'd like to be like a bumblebee but I'm afraid of 'em."

At that moment a car horn sounded and brought me back to the bench in front of the newspaper building. *Isn't that something...but I'll bet Billy is handling his fears better than I am.* In no mood to analyze the flashback and its implications; I stood up, stretched, laughed again, tossed the paper bag into a nearby trash container, and strolled along the north bank river walk of the St. Johns River directly across from Friendship fountain where I proposed to June. *I've only met one Billy, but I've traveled throughout the states and some of Europe...I'm living it up, working in the land of the free, and June and I share one of the most beautiful spots in the world.* The water lapped against the boardwalk and agreed with me so I headed east toward downtown Jacksonville. I glanced across the mighty stream that was about three football fields wide and at the bank where I stood about seventy feet deep. I looked across the river to Friendship Park and prayed, *Oh, Heavenly Father, I thank you so much for June, her level headed approach to life and her deep faith.* I glanced around, picked up a stone and threw it into the current. *There's no way I'm going to sink like that rock back into that addiction. With June at my side and you always with me, Father, my old wounds from the banks and the Rock will be washed away.*

I laughed out loud and quoted a verse of scripture that helped me bridge troubled waters in prison. "For God has not given me a spirit of fear, but of power and of love and of a sound mind."

Feeling better, I turned a canter into a gallop and in a matter of minutes my worries left me. I looked up at the magnificent, new marble skyscrapers before me and felt like I could climb any of them. Like a kid, like Billy from the country, I craned my neck to see the top of several tall buildings under construction. I was especially attracted to a manmade monolith next to the Omni Hotel. Its modern design and grandeur captured my attention. There were no barriers, so I walked up Italian marble steps separating the grand structure from the street and stepped inside. *I'm in a bank: the layout with tellers' windows, a huge vault opposite office cubicles: it's a bank.* I laughed a nervous kind of laughter; my body quivered and adrenalin left my gut and surged upward into my heart causing it to pound like a judge's gavel on his bench. *I'm in a bank unsupervised; I'm deviating and could be violated for breaking parole.* But like a kid, I rationalized that it was not really a bank since it had not opened for business. And I jerked my eyes around to see if anyone was watching me. Though it was not yet in operation, the smell of the place reminded me of the bank where I was shot and arrested four years earlier. *Turn and run,* I told myself, but the curious child in me spurred me on to check out the teller stations, replete with mahogany windows framing slick marble counter tops. Then I smiled and told myself and an imaginary judge, *"This bank already smacks of money, but honestly, Your Honor, I'm not casing this joint; I'm just looking around."*

An elevator door across the lobby opened and construction workers spilled out. *I can take a ride to the top and get a good view of the river and the city.* On the way up, I felt like the fifteen-year-old Kenny Cooper in Logan, West Virginia, rising to the top of a building on an elevator for the first time in his life. This trip to the top was just as exciting, and when I stepped off the elevator, just as rewarding. The bank's design featured huge picture windows that rose to the full length of the walls, which were at least twenty-five feet high.

From that eagle's perch I eyed the breathtaking panorama of the River City. The skyscrapers lining the St. Johns River formed a golden ribbon winding its way northward to the Atlantic Ocean at Mayport. I turned from the window, sauntered over to the west side of the mighty edifice and gazed across the river. I located Friendship Fountain far beneath me and recalled for the second time that hour my proposal to June six months earlier. I raised my hands and thanked God for her, thanked Him for leading me to the city and for helping me land a job at the newspaper. No one was around so I prayed out loud, "Oh God, please help me make it as a writer; I really don't want to fail and go back..."

That nightmarish fear reminded me it was time for me to return to work, so I made my way back to the elevator. I pushed the call button, but no light came on. I tried again with the same result. Panic grabbed me and I breathed a second prayer, *God help me*, but nothing happened. No elevator. *I'm stranded! I'm locked up in a bank.* I laughed like a mad man at that thought and the laughter relaxed me enough to crank my brain into gear. *The stairs; I'll go back down the stairs.* I glanced this way and that. *There are no stairs. There's a door. It's locked. Oh, God, help me.* I returned to the elevator and pushed the button again and again, and waited and waited and waited. *Nothing. I'm locked up in a bank for real. How weird is this? I can't scream for help.* But I did. And no one answered. No one came to rescue me. *Surely the construction workers will come back.* But they didn't and in a half hour that seemed like a day in prison, I realized the workers must have gone for the day and turned the elevator off. "I can hear myself now trying to explain to my parole officer and the work release center why I couldn't report back to work on time."

A voice in my rattled brain said, "The police will have their own take on why a bank robber was hanging out in a bank."

I said out loud, "Coop, get a hold of yourself. They won't think I'm casing this place, studying its design for a later time."

"It's back to the Rock with you," Fear shrieked from somewhere beyond the giant windows.

"Shut up, Fear; shut up!" I screamed.

Then at that moment, it occurred to me to ask God for help again, so I prayed. "Oh, God....I really need your help...send someone to rescue me. Nothing happened. Five minutes passed. Still nothing. I fell to my knees and prayed... and prayed. I felt better but nothing happened...now it's been ten minutes. I opened my mouth to scream again for help when suddenly, without warning a light lit up on the elevator control panel. An elevator was coming up the shaft.

"Thank you, Lord!" I shouted and laughed.

The elevator door opened. A man jumped out, looked at me as his eyes grew wide like my hostages, and shouted, "What in the world!"

I was speechless.

He screamed, "What are you doing here?"

"I work over at the newspaper; was looking around during my lunch break."

"Didn't you see the signs in the lobby?"

I said, "Like a kid, I was just looking around, didn't notice when everyone left. Thank God you came back."

"We weren't going to but ...you're sure lucky I left my lunch box up here."

He disappeared for a moment and returned. Without a word I got on the elevator with him, rode it back down, thanked him for rescuing me, streaked out of the building and speed-walked back to The Florida Times Union.

On the way up the elevator to the second floor where my office was located, I stared at the floor button light on the panel and asked God what my being locked up in a bank building was all about.

"Father, did you allow that to happen so I can deal with fear, maybe my fear of banks, or worse yet, are you trying to tell me a horrible hidden urge to rob a bank still growls inside me?"

Out loud, I said, "Well , Big Dog, you may growl, but you ain't gonna push my elevator buttons anymore! Whine, Big Dog, whine!"

In the weeks that followed, God brought me face to face with fear in ways that not only answered my questions but quelled my anxiety and prepared me for ministering to ex-prisoners like me.

21

Ironically, His first intervention happened the following week at a bank two miles from home. As I walked into the Barnett Bank on Dunn Avenue near Interstate-95 on that sunny afternoon, nothing in the air told me I would experience the fear and frustration a bank customer feels when a bank robbery comes down. In line waiting my turn at the middle of five teller windows three people stood in front of me. Suddenly a commotion in the commercial business line to my right grabbed my attention. I jerked my head around in time to see a young man snatch a money bag from a customer. I couldn't move. My mind wanted to stop him, but my body would not cooperate.

The robber sped past me and burst through the front door. Without thinking, I wheeled around and raced through the door in hot pursuit. When the young man dashed into the busy street, dodging cars, I "slammed on the brakes" and watched from the sidewalk. The sounds of screeching tires, and honking horns agreed with what I was seeing. In the second of five lanes, a white passenger car came to a dead stop to avoid colliding with the robber. Quick as a deer, he leaped over the fender, barely missed being struck by a second car in the next lane, and disappeared into a super market parking lot across the street.

I stood there on the sidewalk bug eyed, talking out loud to myself:

"Why in the world did I chase him?"

142

"No one else did."

"Because I'm the only bank robber?"

"What's that got to do with it?"

"Father," I prayed, *"Part of me wanted to return the money that had been stolen; another part of me wanted to stop him... for his sake."*

As I turned around to go back into the bank, the thought struck me that I chased him because I knew only tragedy lay ahead for him. *"I wanted to spare him from the craziness, the pain, the tragic end he faces. Oh, God, help him. Please spare him from that awful fate."*

Sheepishly, feeling weird and out of place, I looked around to see if anyone was watching me talk to myself like a crazy man. No one was gawking at me, so I returned to the entrance of the bank. And in that surreal moment, past robberies flashed before me: victims' contorted faces, heavy bags of money, handguns, a slug slamming into my chest at the Carrolwood Exchange Bank in Tampa – the end of my criminal rampage. I staggered and almost went down, but in a millisecond I regained my balance, stepped through the front door and walked back into the bank lobby. I muttered, *"Thank God that crazy life is behind me."*

Standing in line, I looked for the victim. He was nowhere to be seen. *They have taken him into an office to help him deal with the trauma and recover from the shock. Oh, my God, I'm so sorry. I hope he's okay.*

Out of the corner of my eye I saw a police car pull up in front of the bank. *This is crazy, Lord, I know I didn't do it, but I feel like they came to arrest me.*

A feminine childlike voice rescued me. "Mr. Cooper... Mr. Cooper!"

It was Amy Beech, the teller letting me know she was ready to serve me. It must have been clear to her that I was disturbed. She expressed her concern. "Are you okay, Mr. Cooper?"

"Yes, I'm fine; but it's hard to believe what just happened."

"I've been a teller for five years, but it always shakes me up. I'll never get used to it."

"I'm so sorry," I said, shocked by the depth of my sorrow.

She looked at me and humor danced in her eyes, "You didn't rob the bank, sir!"

Flashbacks of other tellers at other banks flooded me and robbed me of words.

I must have looked strange to her, so she broke the silence, "Are you sure you're okay?"

"No, I'm not, and someday I'll tell you why I'm not okay with the robbery, Amy."

I yearned to bare my soul and confess to her that she was reaching out to a scumbag bank robber, who had wreaked terror on helpless victims like her, and I wanted to ask her forgiveness. But I didn't.

On the way home to June where I could share how much the experience troubled me, I talked to God about it and repented once more for my wanton disregard for tellers and use of firearms when I robbed banks. Out loud, I said, *"Father, it's me again. What a day! At least the young man didn't use a gun; he just snatched the money bag out of the customer's hand. Hopefully, his close encounter with*

144

death...almost getting killed by those two cars, will serve as a warning of what lies ahead. Surely he didn't get his kicks out of defying death, and take even bigger risks like I did. Oh God, help him... and me; I need you very much."

By the time I reached the house, I had settled down and was able to talk to June more rationally than I had talked to Miss Beech or to God. At the kitchen table, I told her about the flashbacks of robbing banks, the terrorized victims and my emotions.

"June, I relived some to the feelings I experienced robbing banks; it was almost like I was the bank robber."

"I hope you didn't get a rush of adrenalin?"

"Are you serious?"

"No, dummy; I'm trying to get you to lighten up."

"No, thank God. I felt horrible for the victim but also pity for the young man...what he was facing."

June reached over and put her hand on mine. "I've prayed for some time that the Lord would help you work through some of your doubts and fears."

I agreed with her track. "Honey, I believe my being at the bank today was an answer to your prayer."

"What do you mean?"

"I was in the right place at the right time today for God's purpose," I said.

June's eyes told me she wasn't with me. "What was his purpose?"

I laughed and retorted, "That's why I'm talking this out with you – to ask you what you think – to help me sort it out."

"Do you want to know what I think?"

"Probably."

She rolled her eyes. "I believe God wants you to sort through things yourself."

"I don't like the sounds of that."

"I didn't figure you would; Mom tells me I prefer quick easy answers to life's toughest questions, and you may be doing the same thing."

"I am."

"Ken, your recovery is going to take time; the flash-backs, the nightmares you have of banks, of the bloody deaths at prison, getting all that out will not happen over night."

"You sound like a nurse, nurse...thanks for noth-ing... no really, I know you're right. It sure would be good, though, if I felt more okay about myself."

"Let's just keep praying the prayer of St. Charles. God is sure to put you in the right place at the right time for his right purposes."

22

The following day I had an opportunity during my monthly report time to tell Jon Blanchard, my parole officer, about the bank robbery. I relived the episode throughout the night and flashed back to several holdups of my own so sleep evaded me and when I arrived at the parole office, I was a physical and emotional wreck ready to crash. As I waited in the lobby full of ex-convicts, waiting and waiting for him to call me back to Blanchard's office, sweat formed on my forehead and wet the palm of my hands. I stared at the door that led to his office, rubbed my hands together and preached to myself, *I'm more scared than when I robbed banks...but it's no wonder, Coop: Mr. Blanchard hasn't liked you from day one...he's vowed to prove I'm a phony, a jail house Christian he will send back to prison.*

Half awake, half asleep, I stared at the floor and continued the inner conversation: *Why couldn't he be like Carol Norman, Rick Hughes and Dick Morris? They believe in me...this guy hates my guts for some reason and's out to get me...send me back to prison.*

"Kenneth Cooper! Cooper," came a voice from nowhere..."Cooper, wake up!"

It was the dreaded voice of disgust and venom spewed from those prison guards who loathed inmates. I jerked my body straight at attention and prepared to shout out my department of corrections number like I had done hundreds of times in prison during Count Time when the prison staff counted each inmate to make sure we were all present and accounted for.

"Cooper! Cooper!" the voice came again,

"087868, Sir!" I belched out.

Laughter erupted around me and stirred my senses. Mr. Blanchard and the ex-prisoners seated about me had heard my "count-time" nightmare blunder and broken into uproarious laugher when I yelled out my prison number.

"You're not back there, yet, Cooper," Mr. Blanchard announced with a sarcastic, negative tone.

Adrenaline rushed into my brain and a flood of thoughts streamed through me, but no words would form on my lips. Anger, embarrassment and shame choked them, and things became worse a few minutes later when I sat down in my parole officer's office. "Did you have anything to do with the Barnett Bank robbery yesterday," he asked.

I felt like my heart would burst as it pumped fear into my gut, and through my body. My animal instinct was to attack him...at least with words, but somehow I managed to use my head and respond like a normal citizen who had never entertained robbing a bank much less robbed one. "I couldn't believe my eyes; the robbery was a complete surprise, yeah, it really shook me up..."

Mr. Blanchard interrupted me: "What do you mean shook up; how did you feel, Cooper?" His clipped words and look of morbid satisfaction and curiosity took me back to the faces of inmates who had just witnessed a rape or murder in prison.

"I felt violated...sir!"

"Now, you know how your victims felt, Cooper."

148

I hated the venom in his voice as he hissed my name, but to my surprise, I said, "Especially those I took hostage from the banks...I'll never get over it."

Indignation flushed his face, "How do you think they're handling it?"

"I pray for them, sir...and ask people to pray for me, too, sir."

"Well, I don't know about that...robbers almost always rob again."

A nervous laughter came up out of me, and I blurted, "Sir, I steer clear of banks when I can."

He got the weak joke, grunted, eyed me coldly and tapped the pen in his hand on the desk separating us but didn't say anything else. I knew the conversation had come to a close. I stood up and took a step toward the door. The little boy in me couldn't leave well enough alone, so I turned and said, "I'll steer clear of banks, sir...even river banks."

This time he smirked and told me he would see me next month *if not before at the bank.* I laughed at his humor, and on the way home, as I passed the bank that had been held up, I asked the Lord to continue to strengthen my resolve to never rob again, and to soften Mr. Blanchard's heart to believe I was sincere in my effort to abide by the law and actually do things to improve life for myself and others.

The way God chose to "strengthen my resolve" shocked me. It happened at the very same bank a week later. It appeared that he used Satan to test me to see how serious my vow was.

Like the first incident, it burst upon me like an explosion. Entering the bank, sudden movement to my right, toward the safety vaults, grabbed my attention. I glanced that way and was astonished by what I saw: a table laden with stacks of green backs in the doorway, a woman dashing away from it toward me. I stopped. She flew by, but as she passed I caught a quick look at her face. It was pale with a green tint, and her expression told me she was quite nauseous. Her hand over her mouth confirmed it. She was running to the bath room to throw up. I glanced back toward the table of money. *It's half way in! Half way out of the vault! Unattended!* It amazed me that the table was only three steps from me, and out of sight of the bank employees, including the tellers.

I laughed and said, *"Satan, you are a liar; you're the thief and I will not fall for your trick."*

I dashed around the corner to the teller station, told the first teller about the problem and pointed back toward the vault. I shouted, "Come, see!"

She looked at me with upraised eyebrows but didn't respond.

"There's a bunch of money on a table around the corner," I said through gritted teeth.

"Oh my word!" she shouted, excused herself from her customer, bolted over to the table, pushed it into the vault and slammed the heavy door shut.

She turned to me and said, "Thank you...thank you, sir!"

"You're quite welcome...in my professional opinion there must have been eighty thousand on that table."

She looked perplexed. ""Probably...you're in the banking business?"

To my amazement, I said, "I used to be."

She had no idea, of course, what I was talking about and said, "It's a great job...this kind of thing just doesn't happen...did you enjoy it."

I laughed. "Immensely!"

"I didn't mean this crazy incident...banking."

"That too, and Lord willing, I'll tell you about it some time."

"Please do, sometime...now back to work."

I followed her back to the tellers' windows and waited my turn, but I couldn't stop smiling and mumbling to myself, "Coop, you are one crazy dude; why in the world did you say that?" Do I have a need to talk about robbing a bank; I'd better not do it here."

That thought sobered me up, and though still in shock, I managed to stand before a teller and take care of business. When I returned to the car in the parking lot, I got in and sat down, but didn't start the engine. I just sat there. It took me several minutes to recover enough to turn the key in the ignition. When the engine cranked, I said out loud, "What was that all about?"

"I could have grabbed thousands, stuffed it in my shirt and been gone in seconds, and no one would have seen me."

"What a trap?" And then I opened my trap about being a bank robber.

"That whole thing was set up just for me!"

"Incredible."

Finally, I relaxed. When I did, a wave of laughter swept upon me. I laughed and laughed. In between gasps for air, I asked God if this was His doing?"

"Father, was this some kind of weird test?"

Of course there was no answer.

"Yes, that was a test and the cool thing is I passed."

"Like I told Mr. Blanchard, *I'm different. I'm not crazy or controlled by that hunger to play Superman, or grab the quick, easy money any more."*

At that moment, a woman parked her car next to mine and stared at me as I continued to talk to myself.

I smiled at her and kept right on talking. *"I don't care; God is helping me work through this stuff, my fear, doubts about whether I've really changed."*

Two days later the Lord provided yet another lesson in his crash course on adjusting to life outside prison. It came through Raymond Duncan, director of Time for Christ Prison Ministry. He reached out to me at *the Rock* when I was serving a ninety-nine year sentence. Through his ministry, Time for Christ, with the help of Jim Whyte, he convinced the Florida Parole Commission I was a changed man who was no longer a threat to society. With their help I walked out of prison in less than four years.

When he called and asked me to serve as the guest speaker for a ministry fundraiser, I was delighted to do something for the two men most responsible for my freedom, but I worried that the bank incidents had rattled me enough that I would be too nervous to speak in a way that would benefit Raymond's ministry.

On the way down the elevator in the newspaper office, Mr. Whyte talked about things that rescued me from my nerves. We talked about the wedding and how June and I were doing, but he didn't ask me how I was adjusting to life outside prison. When we arrived at the Independent Life building, a twenty-eight floor tower on the St. John's River in the heart of downtown Jacksonville, where the meeting would occur, he parked in the basement and led me to the elevator.

As the door opened he touched me on the shoulder and said, "I understand that you have an affinity for elevators in bank buildings."

I mused. "I hope Miss Simmons didn't snitch me out."

"I'm just teasing...that must have been scary."

"Really, no more than zooming to the top of this building to speak to a group of bankers and..."

Jim interrupted me with laughter. "Yes, the chairman of the Barnett Bank is eager to meet you."

I thought of Moe's song, and the line "the bankers, police and people in the church pew played in my mind and my heart "dropped" three floors when I relived the recent incidents at the bank, but I hung on to say, "I'm not ready for this."

"What do you mean?" He asked.

I avoided the bank incidents and said, "One of my buddies wrote a song about this moment."

Mr. Whyte looked concerned, but ignored my statement and said, "You'll like Hugh Jones; he's a great friend of mine who will like you."

I needed to talk out my feelings and said, "It's surely not because he's a banker but what's going on in my life."

He sniffed and asked, "What do you mean by that, Ken?"

At that moment we arrived at the top floor. When the elevator door opened, I knew it was not the time nor place to vent, so I said, "I wasn't prepared for such a fast rise to the top though it had been predicted by two men in prison."

Jim frowned, caught me by the shoulder and pulled me over to the side of the elevator lobby, "Are you okay, Ken?"

"Probably not, but let's walk over to that giant picture window for a minute." I said as I pointed to a huge window overlooking picturesque downtown Jacksonville.

When we arrived and looked out over the St. John's River, far below, winding its way through the scenic city, without turning to me Jim asked, "What's going on?"

I responded in Hillbilly lingo: "You and I are smack dab in the middle of a prophecy being fulfilled."

"What do you mean by that?"

"I'll read it to you," I said and from my back pocket, pulled out a trusted little Bible given to me in prison by Gideon International and read from Psalm 113:8: "He raises up the poor out of the dust, and lifts the needy out of the dunghill that he may set him with princes, even with the princes of his people."

Jim turned and looked at me with wonder typed across his "editor's" brow, but he didn't say anything.

I rescued him: "In the sticks where I came from we would put it this way: 'I am moving on up from the outhouse to the penthouse.'"

Quick as a cat, Jim Whyte quipped, "In your case you have moved on up from the *Big House* at the Rock to Jacksonville's version of the *Top of the Mark*."

154

I guffawed and said, "You got it boss; the amazing thing is that a man named Nathaniel, on my last night in prison ... he prophesied that I would sit with the princes of the people in a big house."

Jim laughed, grabbed me by the arm and said, "Well, my lad, you're always welcome at the Whyte house, and that prophecy about the princes of Jacksonville is about to come true."

23

Despite the miracle of the prophecy and even though Jim and Raymond tried to prepare me, the setting of the luncheon was overwhelming and I had trouble focusing on the people in the luxuriously appointed room. I excused myself and wandered back over to the window to relax and take in the spectacular view one more time. From the River Room atop the Independent Life building I traced the St. Johns as it wound its way through the River City. And when I turned around and looked at the table where I would sit, and took a step in that direction, "the princes of the people" were seated there. Hugh Jones, Chairman of the Board of Barnett Banks; Ander Crenshaw, U.S. Representative; and Ed Austin, State's Attorney. The sight of three of the most powerful and respected men of the city standing up to meet me staggered me. I felt so unworthy and out of place. But when Raymond moved our way and introduced me as a "staff writer of the Times-Union and a friend of the ministry" I relaxed enough to look them in the eye when we shook hands and said our "How do you dos".

"I understand you're our guest speaker, Ken," said Mr. Austin who was seated to my left at the table just big enough for four. *No wonder I'm nervous; that bulge under his jacket...he's packing iron.*

I stammered, "Y...yes, sir, I write for the Times-Union Neighbor."

"That must be enjoyable; what do you write?" Mr. Crenshaw asked from my right.

"Feature stories...human interest stuff about people in our neighborhoods."

"You need to write about Ed running for Mayor," Mr. Jones said from across the table.

"May I quote him on that, Mr. Austin?" I asked and took my pen in hand as if to write his remarks on the fancy black napkin that graced our white table cloth.

"No, no offense to Hugh," he said, "but prosecuting criminals is not the right background for a mayor."

I choked at the words *prosecuting criminals* and sat there speechless.

Mr. Crenshaw rescued me with his sense of humor and said, "It may be the perfect background."

We all laughed and the laughter seemed to clear my head. I thought about Raymond's plan to introduce me simply as "The Gentleman Bank Robber" and I wanted to prepare them for the shock they would surely feel when I was introduced, so I looked at Mr. Jones and said, "I used to be in the banking business."

His eyes sparkled like new silver dollars. "I'm sure the newspaper business is a lot more enjoyable," he said.

"Yes, but not as profitable."

At that moment Raymond clanged a spoon on a glass to quiet the crowd and asked Ander Crenshaw's brother, Mack, who wore a priest's collar, to bless the food.

While he was praying I said my own prayer to myself: *Help!*

But when it came time for me to get up and speak, a confidence and calm came over me until I heard Raymond's words, "I give you Ken Cooper, a man known in Jacksonville as one of Jim's journalists, but by many more across Florida as the Gentleman Bank Robber."

There was no applause. A stunned silence settled over the room. Finally, I managed to clear my throat and say, "It's true! I used to be in the banking business doing illegal withdrawals but I gave that up."

The crowd roared. Ed Austin stood up and said, "Ken tried to warn us he'd been in the banking business, but we ignored him."

The room burst out again in uproarious laughter and somehow I felt good enough to say, "Yes, I tried to tell them, but I'm glad they didn't pick up on it because Hugh would surely have asked me which of his banks I robbed."

The crowd didn't know whether to laugh or cry at that but I heard many chuckles. I continued: "And I'm telling you right now, before you ask, Mr. Jones, I plead the fifth on the grounds that it might tend to incriminate me, embarrass you... and shake up Mr. Austin."

Again there was uproarious laughter, but Mr. Austin, who was still standing, with a side sweep of his hand, quieted the crowd and said, "I'll ask plenty of questions when Mr. Cooper finishes his talk."

The crowd roared and sweat broke out on my forehead, but I took advantage of the moment, "Representative Crenshaw, this will be a filibuster for the ages."

Not to be outdone, the tall politician who was known to hate filibustering, stood up and declared, "The representative from Florida yields to the bank robber from Kentucky."

Again the *princes of the people* laughed and laughed. I loved the stage that had apparently been set for me by my gracious table hosts with the blessing of God. I stepped forward, raised my hands as if to surrender, bank robbery style, and said, "Please raise your hands:...this is a holdup for the Lord."

The crowd roared and raised their hands. I took control and barked, "Keep your hands up and no one will get hurt..."

The happy victims guffawed again.

In a serious tone I formed my right hand into a pistol. And declared, "For thirteen years I took money with a gun; now, today, I'm here to ask you to willingly support this great ministry, Time for Christ, that underwrites Kairos Prison Ministry that turns men like me from crime to Christ, from robbing banks to holding up unsuspecting, princes of the people...leaders who can join Raymond in doing something about preventing crime in Jacksonville."

With those words the mood became more serious so I said, "Time for Christ and Kairos is all about crime prevention in Jacksonville and Raymond needs to raise more money today than the banks used to cough up to me."

And so it went. Following the meeting both Mr. Austin and Mr. Jones approached me. The prosecuting attorney amazed me when he asked me to visit a former city leader in federal prison, and Mr. Jones asked me to join him for lunch at his office atop the Barnett Bank Tower. It was clear to me that the prophecy of my brothers in prison had come true. I was not only sitting with the princes of the people but had found favor with them. In the days to come, ironically, it became clear that I had not found favor with some people, including family members... and God would give me a glimpse of their hearts.

24

Two weeks later when I visited my Brother, Paul, who lived in Ocala, two hours south of Jacksonville, I wasn't given a glimpse of family rejection; I was offered a full heartfelt eye-full that would shape the way I would see family and affect my relationship with my kid brother the rest of his life.

Given permission from Mr. Blanchard to spend a Sunday lunch with Paul, June and I drove down for what could have been a grand occasion. Some of his children and grandchildren, most of them red-headed like him, were there and we talked about "old times" when we were younger and all five of us brothers were alive. He showed me around his mini ranch and pointed out all the things that he had done to the place. He was especially proud of his horses and chickens and the close moment with him stirred up hope in me that we could recover the old bond that once made us inseparable. Nevertheless, I felt he was holding back from expressing some of the things going on in his gut.

After the tour of his place he invited June and I to join him for lunch at a restaurant near his home. We enjoyed a good lunch, though a tension in the air bothered me. After lunch, in the parking lot, the stuff inside him that created the heavy atmosphere began to come out. When I thanked him for lunch and told him I would come back down in a few weeks with a friend I wanted him to meet, the look on his face took a strange twist. "So long as it's not an-other ex-convict, I guess it would be okay," he said.

"What do you mean...am I the only ex-con welcome at your place?"

"Well, really, the reason I'm meeting with you here today is..."

I interrupted him, "I'm actually not welcome either?"

"Sad to say; that's true....I don't want to feel like I have to lock up everything tight."

"Well I'm sure glad you told me; the friend I wanted you to meet is not a bank robber; he's my new son, Floyd... June's son."

Paul dropped his eyes and pressed the tips of his fingers against his lips as if he were in deep thought or didn't want to express what was brewing inside."

Anger boiled up in me, my face became rigid and my words clipped: "Let's make sure I've got this right, little brother; no ex-prisoner, whether he's innocent of his crime or not, is welcome in your home."

He gripped his hands into white knuckled fists and his tight lips retorted, "That's right!"

I objected to his judgment. "Floyd's my son; he's in-nocent -- it really hurts that you don't want to meet him."

"It's better this way," he said as he turned away to head toward his pickup truck.

I extended my hand to block his path. "What could possibly be good about this?"

He brushed my arm aside and snapped, "It'll keep you guys from getting shot!"

"You'd shoot us?" I shouted angrily. "You'd actually shoot us!"

His red face turned crimson and he formed a gun with his right hand, pointing the "barrel- finger" up into my face, "I'll shoot you on sight!"

June tugged at my arm in an attempt to get me to walk away, but I ignored her and said, "Paul, you'll live to regret this day!"

"For Mother's sake don't you dare come around! Do you understand? You know I'll shoot you!"

"Yes, Paul, I know you would!"

"You've been warned; never set foot on my property again!"

I laughed a sick kind of laughter that stuck in my throat. "I'm not about to get myself killed, brother!"

"That's a good thing for mother," he said as he turned and marched toward his pickup truck.

I took one step to follow him, stopped in my tracks and yelled, "People do change you know."

He just stared at me, got into his truck and drove away.

I turned to June and said, "Honey; he's my little brother; I may never see him again."

"Brother, or not; you must let him go."

"Oh, I am, it hurts, but he'd shoot me!"

"He really means it?"

"Yes, if I set my foot on his property," I said, took her by the hand and walked with her to our car.

As the restaurant disappeared in the rear view mirror, I said through tears, "My little brother...my little brother would shoot me; he blames me for mother's stroke and bad health."

June became pensive, opened her hands into a question mark and asked, "Why, Ken, what is this all about, really?"

"Probably; it goes back to mother's failing health...the stroke she had shortly after she saw me on TV carried out of the bank on a stretcher."

"What a scene...what a shock to her...he blames you?"

"Yes, I can understand that and don't blame him."

"Maybe that's why he warned you...remember he said 'for Mother's sake, don't you dare do it!'"

"No doubt."

"I sure wouldn't want to walk in his shoes."

"Yes, that's a heavy load of anger and unforgiveness he's totin' ... much heavier than a '45!"

At that point, before we got back on Interstate Seventy-Five to return to Jacksonville, I pulled over to the side of the road and asked June to pray with me. June closed her eyes with me, and we held hands as I cried out to God, "Oh my God, I'm so sorry for the mess I've made, so many people hurt...please bring the family and me together. Oh, Lord, please let it stop here; no more people hurt...help me resist the temptation to try Paul; I don't want to get shot, but please allow me to reach out to him in some way. Bless him to know you personally, if he doesn't, so you can enable him to forgive me."

The return trip to Jacksonville enabled us to sort through the recent experiences, but our discussion didn't prepare us for what was to happen next.

25

Two days after I returned from the dreadful encounter with Paul, Becky called from her home near Detroit, where she moved from Louisville to accept a part time job as a model. After she let me know about the move and the opportunity to work in Detroit, she told me she was really upset with her uncle Paul and other family members who couldn't accept me back into the clan. "Dad, the family is like a *house-divided* over you. Half of our relatives seem to accept you with a forgiving spirit while the other half appear to have turned their backs on you and don't want anything to do with you."

In an attempt to lighten her mood, and at the same time expel feelings of anger and shame balled up in my gut, I laughed and said, "Becky, the only thing I can't forgive them for is putting a high fashion model like you smack-dab in the middle."

She returned the laughter and said, "What makes you think I'm a model in the middle, Pops?"

I sighed into the phone and said, "Girl, you've got me there; I'm the guilty one in the middle."

To console me, she said, "It's like the stuff that goes through my mind when someone comes against Kenny or one of our three kids."

Before answering I thought about who my daughter had become and how close we were despite my criminal past and being separated by eighteen-hundred miles. In my two years of freedom, though we talked on the phone quite often, I had driven with June to their home in Louisville only once. During that glorious reunion, where I introduced her to my bride, I discovered that my little girl, now twenty-five, had become a dedicated woman of God whose heart's desire was to serve the Lord and take care of her family. A gifted musician like her mother, Jennie, and maternal grandfather, Walter Regal, she also served her Heavenly Father and family through singing, and playing the piano in church.

In an attempt to use humor that would grab her to change the subject, I said, "Sounds like a song you, your mom and granddad would write and then put to music, violin and piano, my dear!"

She sighed and said, "Dad, don't try to patronize me when I am dead serious and..."

I interrupted my daughter like a child refusing to encourage his mother's maternal instincts, and in jest ranted and raved: "You may be my big Sister in Christ since you were born again at eight, fifteen years before I committed my life to Christ at forty-five, but, my girl who is acting like my mother, I've got a solution..."

Becky laughed and laughed so loudly I paused in my spiel until she quieted down. Then with a competitive challenge in my tone, I said, "Let's meet midway between Florida and Michigan, at mom's place in Kentucky. We'll invite all the kin folks and have it out right there in the middle of everybody; and then I'll go home to live with you, Mom."

After more uncontrollable laugher, Becky said, "Dad, you're impossible, but I do like your idea. Kenny and I will take you and Mama June on; besides, the kids, Kenny and I are dying to see you."

"Great; it's settled then," I said.

She continued with the last word: "And we'll meet you in Kentucky if you promise to follow us back home after we defeat you two in hoops."

"It's a deal; we'll stop and visit Mom—she'll love that, and you tell Kenny Ferguson that if he'll bring the basketball, I'll bring hoops shoes for June and me... the Coopers and the Fergusons will have it out right there."

"You're on, Dad...but you're kidding me, right?"

"No, I'm dead serious, both about meeting you at mom's and the two couples going head to head in a game of round ball to decide this thing once and for all."

She laughed and then set a date when we could commiserate and recreate.

Three weeks later on a Saturday afternoon the family duel occurred on a basketball court located in a recreation area at Cumberland Falls State Park, about twenty-five miles north of Mother's home place. It was dad and mom against daughter and son-in-law, or as we said, the Kentucky Wildcats versus the Michigan Wolverines in a half-court ten-bucket contest. The only rules were "make-it take it," and "straight back up with a rebound" to balance the age difference of twenty-five years between the rivals.

Really, I figured the two teams were evenly matched since June was in great shape and had played *first-five* on her high school basketball teams while Becky, Kenny and I had not, but they were both agile and hostile young athletes who had proven in track and basketball that they could compete at a high level.

167

With trash talk befitting a civil war battle between Yankees and Rebels, and too many belly laughs, we clawed and scratched our way to a nine-to-nine-bucket tie after thirty minutes of competition. The team that scored the next basket would win the contest.

I called time out to give the team from the South a chance to re-Coop while the young Fergies caught their breath. Laughing, they taunted us by doing wind sprints around and around us as June and I put our heads together to plan our next and final play.

"Sweetheart, I'm winded...we've got to score on this possession or..."

"Don't worry about a thing, gramps; I'll throw the ball into you, move toward you and set up a screen on Kenny at the top of the key. We'll do a pick and roll past him and Becky so you can toss the ball over them to me as I cut to the basket."

The plan worked to perfection except for the imperfection of the plan. When I attempted to lob the ball over Becky's head, she exploded like a rocket and swatted the ball toward the out-of-bounds line under the basket. But quick as a Cat, June dove through the air, and while suspended between heaven and earth, knocked the orange orb back across the boundary line into my hands. As if in slow motion, I saw June crash face first on the gravel surrounding the concrete court, but in that instant I caught the ball and twisted it into the rim. As it passed through the goal it made the sweetest "string music" I'd heard since prison.

Laughing like a loon, I joined June in the unforgiving gravel and rolled down the hill with her. "We won! We won!" I shouted above her laughter. It amazed me that she found amusement in her bloody mess. In her gravel pitted right hand she held a dental implant that said more to me than words could as they asked the question I expected to come out of June's bloody mouth: "Hey, big boy, which do you care more about? Winning, or your wife?"

26

The next morning, June and I woke up early, dragged my aching bones out of bed, loaded up the car and hit the road for Michigan, knowing we would arrive a day behind Becky and Kenny, who returned home right after the basketball classic. But we made a quick stop at a local dentist's office in Whitley City, had the implant repaired, and headed out from there for Becky's.

In no hurry, we took scenic US 27 northward and drove about ten miles to Parker's Lake near the junction of Kentucky 90 where we visited Natural Arch, one of the Blue Grass State's lesser known nature sites, though it is located only about 25 miles southwest of the well known Cumberland Falls State Park, site of the Cooper-Ferguson basketball showdown, and a magnificent forty foot water fall of the Cumberland river that produces a multi-colored moon-bow at certain times of the year.

We chose the less public, but equally romantic hideaway. To get to the Arch we hiked a short way on a winding trail embraced by giant hemlock pines, pin oaks and tulip poplars graced by a variety of ferns and lichen who shared the dreamy moment with us. As we reclined on a soft-as-down bed of moss only mother-nature could have made up for us that morning, we laughed like a little boy and girl who had discovered a secret place known only to them.

Several smooches and hugs later we returned to the trail and walked hand-in-hand to a picnic table beneath the scenic wonder, placed a cooler crammed with a treat mom had prepared for us. But we couldn't focus on food, not even mother's picnic lunch, though we were hungry.

We were caught up in each other and in nature: the sweet smell of the hemlocks, the harsh aroma of pine resin, the perfume of Sweet Williams, my favorite mountain flower. I held June in my arms for a long moment and then pointed upward toward the top of the mountain. We were awestruck by a majestic sand colored rock arch that spanned what looked like a thirty by sixty foot goose egg shaped opening in a fifty-foot cliff. The Natural Arch seemed to guard the mountaintop and embrace us. But, at the same time, the wonder of the site stirred up questions about the dynamic forces of wind and water that must have formed it, and how long it took the wind to penetrate the cliff and carve the huge hole out of the rock.

Our discussion about the powerful forces of nature took me back to an adventure with a family headed up by an ex-convict that lived in an arch-like cave some twenty miles west of the mountain where we stood. The wind and water had eaten away the same kind of limestone and sand rock formation to form Parker Jack's den where he lived for the duration of the harsh Kentucky winters.

In sharing that experience with June, though, I held on to the punch line about the ex-con living in a cave. To begin my story, I pointed to the west, and with a hillbilly twang said, "Junebug, over yonder about fifteen ridges and jest as many hollers is the old home place of an ex-con, a mountain man named Parker Jack."

My quick thinking, wide-eyed wife from the plains of southwest Georgia squeezed my hand and said, "Arrested for stillen moonshin, no doubt, back in them thar hills."

I laughed. "Well, yes, my Georgia Peach who shouldn't know so much about such things... or about a mountain man who lost his freedom when revenuers caught wind of his private still."

"You're leaving out the high jedge's take on the whole matter, no doubt?"

"No doubt, but what intrigued me about Mr. Jack is that until the government interfered, he was free to live during the summer months in a cabin with his wife and two kids, but when the cold winds of winter blew, he chose to retreat into a nice warm cavern carved out of the mountain by nature."

June's sky blue eyes grew wider, but she attempted to hide her curiosity: "Just a tall tale, my mountain man?"

"No, Jack as I called him, was for real, a little eccentric maybe when it came to the way he chose to live, but some twenty years ago when I last visited him, I had to walk about five miles through the deep woods from the last gravel road. It was worth every step because the king shared his kingdom, his family's old home place including the cave with me."

"An old home place with a cave, that's a wonderful story; tell me more, Ken," June said snuggling closer under my arm, ignoring the cooler stuffed with food and drinks.

"I thought his primitive lifestyle would make a good story for someone, but decided not to follow through with it once I got to know him."

"How's that?"

172

I snickered and said, "I was afraid he would shoot me, but worse yet I didn't want to mess up his life, his way of doing things."

"His privacy, his freedom, maybe?"

"Yeah, he didn't believe in modern ways: electricity, education; he lived real primitive, worked with mules, rode a mule or walked twenty miles out to town for supplies."

"Were his wife and kids okay with that lifestyle?" June asked as she opened the cooler and began to take out our lunch.

"Yep, she was of the same mind, couldn't read nor write, didn't think they needed book larnin to live a good life."

"They had no neighbors? Did they socialize in town, church?"

"No, they preferred to stay to them-selves...worshipped God in their cabin, in the cave or among the trees, ate off the land, had their own cow, mules, chickens, plus all the wild game they wanted. Guess they didn't need much else."

"I've never heard of anyone so independent."

"You're right, but it didn't' set well with the authorities."

"How's that?"

"The first time I visited, when I came out of the woods up through the fields into his garden, he greeted me with a very unfriendly shotgun, apparently panicked that I was a revenuer, or local government official."

"That must have been scary."

"It was; when I saw him leap out from behind an apple tree in front of his wooden house, I took a snapshot with my brain. I'll never forget the picture."

"I can almost see him now," June enthused.

I smiled. "The main feature of the fortyish looking wiry-built fellow in faded bib overalls was a full beard from ear to ear, that formed a spectacular black and silver laced cascade of hair that fell from his face to the bibs of his overalls."

"That wasn't a scary sight?"

"Well, yes and no. When he jumped out from nowhere, A-juice surged from my belly to my brain. And in the split second it took me to see his distorted face and long shotgun pointed at me, fear took over but still there remained a vestige of reasoning in my brain. It ruled and said to my gut, *I might fear him but looks like he fears me more. He thinks I'm the law come to arrest him again for moonshinin', and like before, carry off his family.*"

June was silent, but her glazed eyes with dilated pupils spoke a thousand words of wonder mixed with fear. Her look reminded me of one of the bank teller hostages.

I blinked at that flashback but continued, "The wild-looking man's wide stance with the long gun's barrel pointing at me told me he would defend himself and his family to the death."

Rather than turning tale and running, though, I told my adversary the truth, though it sounded stupid: "Mr. Jack," I squeaked, "I came to hear you play and sing some music."

He laughed like a mad man and chortled, "Ye ain't the revenuer or gov'mint I thought ye war, then?"

"No sir re bob," I shouted and then added, "My recent dead daddy played the mandolin so ah come to hear ye."

"Ye shore look like bad news, but I believe ye," he said as he lowered the gun and told me to "come on in, I reckon."

June slumped down on the picnic table bench and said, "Wow, what an experience. Tell me more."

"Jack lived so far back in the wilderness that it was rumored that his two kids had never been to town, much less to school."

"Oh, I get it now; he thought you were the law that had arrested him for making moonshine, but the real problem: the government considered his kids neglected."

Mixing in mountain lingo, I said, "Ye hit the nail on the head, Ms. Social Worker; it wasn't the moonshine that done him in; in our society, the gov'mint may turn its back, but there are certain things we are bound to do, and many things we aren't free to do as spelled out by those who carry the big stick."

June laughed and said, "Stop that backwoods talk, Mr. Sociology Professor, but here's what I'm thinking: he might have been the king in his kingdom, but he didn't have the right to shoot you with that shotgun though you were trespassing."

I laughed. "Exactly, but he kept it close during the first two visits, then on the third, his firearm gave way to a mandolin when he picked up my favorite instrument jest like yur daddy's, and shared some original music he had wrotten, words and lyrics about his mountain kingdom—the king shared it with me!"

June chuckled, but her face took on a serious look. "He had a good heart; whatever happened to them?"

"Jack finally gave in and arranged for the kids to go to school, but when *they* found out the children lived uner a cliff, *they* made them reside in the cabin all the time."

"I can tell you the end of your tall tale: the Jack family almost froze to death the next winter when they tried to live in the cabin on the windy mountaintop, so *they* moved closer into town where they lived miserable ever after."

27

I guffawed loudly at my wife's insight into the situation and what had actually happened. My laughter must have attracted some of the locals, who gathered in to share our lunch.

Among our would be guests, who wanted to join us for a feast, was a gray flying squirrel that swooped down from a hemlock tree to check out the meal we were spreading out on the table. With him scurried in a posse of chipmunks, who stood at a distance on their haunches and begged for a tidbit with their big brown eyes and tiny paws. I couldn't blame them. I could hardly wait to tear into the ham and cheese sandwiches with tomato, lettuce and mayo...no onions for kissing sweet breath... topped by apples slices covered with peanut butter, and for dessert, mom's homemade fig jam and real cow butter on ginger bread. For June, mom snuck in some cornbread and fresh buttermilk. Food fit for any old-timey mountain boy and flatland country girl.

After a quick blessing that included our little forest friends who had inched closer to *say amen*, we enjoyed the luscious lunch and I washed it down with fresh homemade lemonade made just for me. *What a wonderful mother!*

When we finished dining, we told our new friends goodbye, and as we drove toward Rebecca's place on Interstate-75 that would take us through Lexington, Kentucky, we talked about Parker Jack and how he was just as happy in his little kingdom with his work mules as the "kings" who own their huge bluegrass race horse farms. But the conversation took an unexpected twist when June said, "I think you're fascinated by Mr. Jack's independent spirit that got him in trouble."

"I refuse to respond to that on the grounds that it may tend to incriminate me, Ken Lucky of Kentucky." I said, without taking my eyes off the road.

June smirked, sighed loudly, and said, "Well, there is that side of it, *Your Highness*, but I'm thinking about the love some people have for their home land and family."

"Wow, Mrs. Cooper, you've made my day," I said as I took her soft hand in mine for a moment and asked, "Will you marry me?"

"No!" she said with her mouth, but her eyes said, "Yes!"

I laughed and said, "Love and family; that's exactly why I loved telling people about Kentucky, the ultimate residence or vacation place for families."

June laughed, "Yes, but what about the horses?"

"Darling, I'm no longer into pretty horses and fast women."

She grinned, ignored my bad humor and said, "Mr. High and Mighty, you never were into horseback riding that much, right?"

"Correct, but back to the fast horses, there's nothing more beautiful than a colt galloping across a bluegrass pasture beside his mother."

"Don't be silly, I know that's the logo for the Kentucky Horse Park on that cap perched behind the back seat."

"When I worked for the state, one of the artists on the staff designed and drew it."

"I love it; it's a perfect picture of their relationship and running free!"

"Thank you, 'tis perfect."

"But that old worn out cap is not perfect anymore."

"Why do you think I'm taking you to the Kentucky Horse Park today?"

June laughed. "To get yourself a new cap, brag about your promo and buy me one, too!"

"Yep, exactly, I'm so proud of that picture, the logo of the mare with her colt running."

My Georgia girl who said she loved big brown eyed cows more than horses was not disappointed with the horse park, especially not with the fifty minute horseback ride through the park's deciduous tree forests that brag of blue-grass meadows alongside lazy brooks, begging us to cross over on our easy riders whose hooves knew every stone in the gray native limestone bridges. It intrigued and tickled me that June swayed along on a blond Tennessee Walking mare while I was jostled by a big red Standard Bred stallion that I admitted was too much horse for me.

The ride culminated our enchanted six-hour visit where we watched horses do everything from breeding to giving birth to being laid to rest in a cemetery near statues of the spectacular Man of War and the greatest race horse of all time, Secretariat.

We could talk of little else than our grand experience during a six-hour trip from the horse country through northern Kentucky, across the Ohio River at Cincinnati, and through southern Ohio to Dayton, where we enjoyed supper with Wayne Ball, my cousin, who like thousands upon thousands of Bluegrass State natives had moved across the "Jordan River" to live, work, raise their families and worship God in the "Promised Land."

The next day, after taking in the Wright Brother's Memorial Park and the National Museum of the U.S. Air Force near Wayne's home, my heart yearned to join Orville and Wilbur and zoom on up to Becky's at Detroit, but reality and June made me stick to the ground and almost the speed limit on the drive to my Rebecca's house.

When Becky met us at her front door, I felt as if Jennie, who passed away at twenty-nine, had returned to life. Though it had been just twenty-four hours since I'd seen her, in that moment, it seemed that I was seeing my grown child for the first time.

Before me stood a gorgeous woman with her mother's sparkling hazel eyes although her face beamed with a huge smile that looked like mine in a mirror. I felt complete and didn't want to ever be separated from Becky.

I thought, *I miss you so much, my princess; you must move your family to Florida,* but wisdom told me not to say it out loud.

"June and Dad; don't just stand there looking at me; welcome, come on in," she said.

I didn't budge and sized her up again, saying, "You look so much like your mom, like a Regal, standing there, but you're about six inches taller."

Becky smirked, "Being a five-foot-eight Regal married to a Ferguson didn't help me beat you in basketball; how's your implant, Mama June?"

June laughed, spread her mouth into a thin line with her index fingers, and forced words out through her teeth: "Good as new, bring it on Wolverines... Wildcats are in the house."

We all laughed and Becky said, "I'm so glad you're here, come on into the living room, and we'll sit and talk..."

"No sitting just yet, where's the three urchins, babe," I asked as I looked around for the grandchildren.

"Out playing; they couldn't wait inside for you any longer...come on in the kitchen; there's coffee for the Coopers."

At that moment, the back door burst open and in rushed the kids in question: JP, Javonna and Lee, like *stairsteps* of nine, seven and five. All three surged into my open arms and almost bowled me over. I felt like that was a good idea for the occasion, so I let go and let it happen. The kids loved my antics as I rug wrestled with them and challenged the two boys to take me on, two against one, in arm wrestling. Of course they "won" but middle-sister had been left out of our little boys' game.

She grabbed me by the hand, looked up into my eyes with her large Regal eyes, called me Papa, stole my heart, and led me into their play room where she showed me a doll house, dolls and other major attractions and toys. *I'm in heaven; oh my how much I missed these children... family in lockup. Thank God, I'm free.*

After Javonna's turn, the boys challenged me to a game of basketball and as some country folks would put it, they drubbed me badly in Horse. Sister rooted for the brothers' team. For their victory all three were treated to candy and bubble gum stashed in the storage compartment between the seats of my station wagon.

With Double Bubble in six happy little hands we returned to the play room for a bubble blowing contest that, of course included Papa, who was happy to lose again, when to the delight of the three angels, a huge bubble of sticky tacky gum burst and covered my big nose. The children rolled over on the floor, hysterical.

By the time Kenny came home from work, the kids settled down and sat big eyed as the Kentucky Wildcats teased the Michigan Wolverines about their resounding defeat in our recent basketball game and relived it until our host said, "No mas; no mas!" It was all fun but when we retreated to the piano where Becky played old hymns and some new songs as the rest of us sang along with her. Nothing could have been finer except heaven, until Lee tugged on my shirt sleeve and asked, "Papa, did you really rob banks?"

I almost fainted but laughed and rubbed his tow head when I remembered that JP asked me the same question at the age of four when the family visited me in prison. Reliving that embarrassing moment gave me a little time to figure out how to respond. I looked at Becky and Kenny to get their silent permission to proceed, then said, "Lee, I'm glad you asked me though it makes me feel ashamed...I did rob banks, but I asked God and your parents and a lot of other people to forgive me."

Lee's face glowed, but he didn't say anything so I continued, "They have accepted my apology—do you know what that big word means, Lee?"

"Yes, it means you did something wrong and you say you're sorry and won't do it again."

After his parents and I laughed and told him he explained it well, I made eye contact with Lee, then Javonna and JP, hung my head and said, "I'm sorry and promise I'll never do anything crazy like that again, okay."

To the disappointment of their parents, the kids didn't respond until JP touched my nose and said, "Hey, Papa, let's all blow some more nose bubbles!"

We all guffawed and the laughter relieved the load of guilt pressing me down. The rest of the visit was just as uplifting and fun as that first evening, but when we pulled out of their driveway to head south on the third day, to my amazement a huge rainbow formed in the western sky and reminded me of my deep desire to see Becky and Kenny move south to Florida. Tears wet my eyes as joy rose up in my heart and shouted, "They're coming home!"

June didn't know what was going on inside me, so she placed a warm hand on my arm to comfort me.

"God put a rainbow in the cloud to promise me we will all be one big happy family in Jacksonville."

"I hope Becky will move south soon for the family's sake."

"I hope it's not a sin to pray for it to happen."

June giggled, and said, "No. but let's keep on praying for dad and mom."

"Okay."

"It seems like mom is coming around so surely Dad is going to loosen up, too."

"Nothing could make me happier."

28

Back home, when we heard from Mother Marchant that Dad Marchant had not changed his negative take on our marriage, reality hit us that it might take quite a while for him to come around. As I stood by watching, feeling helpless and to blame, the truth of our circumstance pierced June like a double edged sword that separated her from her father. What made the wound deeper for me was her suffering.

During our first months of marriage, June and I prayed daily asking God to move in his heart to accept me, but in all those months though we lived on the same property and would see each other at a distance, absolutely nothing had changed, so it was hard for June to not lose hope.

But on the morning of April 21 a glimpse of what would occur came to us before we left home for work. It jumped off the page of our Schuller devotional when we discussed the theme for the day, "Trust your past to God."

We focused on the narrative which read:

"All of the mental patients kept repeating, 'If only, if only, if only.' Those words cause mental sickness. These people must learn to say, 'next time... next time... next time.' These words point to the future, to a new day, to healing and health.'"

In closing, as June and I prayed, I cried out to God, asking him to help me get over my past: "I'm willing clay, I know I have serious flaws, but you're the Potter, Father God; please finish the work you began at *the Rock*; please heal the cracks in my character; restore me and help June's father and mother know that I'm not some kind of crackpot bound to ruin their daughter's life."

After the *Amen*, June took me in her arms, dabbed at my tears like a loving mother, but teased me like a tantalizing wife. She purred, "Pottery has always been one of my favorite things...especially crackpots, so surely Mom and Dad will make you a favorite pot, too."

Apparently regressing into my childhood, I gooed like a baby soaking in a warm bath of soothing body wash and said, "You're right, Mom, the only problem is you are not your mother and your father."

"Thank God for that!" she said as she slipped away from me, picked up her lunch and headed for the door to go to work.

Home from work that day, I didn't want her to go and called out, "It's really hard living here right under their feet on these three acres. So please ask God to help me forgive your parents for disliking a likable guy like me who lives right under their nose, on the same plot of land."

Ironically the Lord used mowing the grass on the three acres to answer our prayers. June's parents owned a riding lawn mower that a hired hand used to mow the back acre of the property where they lived in an upstairs garage apartment.

That left the front two acres around our home for me to mow. Though it took me an hour a day in the Florida heat, I mowed the grass with a small push mower. Due to the small area covered by the twenty-four inch cut, given the north Florida climate, by the end of the week when I finished cutting the two acres, it was time to start over again. It bothered me that her dad would watch me from his perch high above me, and I asked God continually to forgive me for my hurt feelings, especially when he was sitting on the shady porch drinking a cold drink.

As I struggled to push the mower through the tough Bermuda grass, the truth of the morning devotional appeared in the green mat before me. I'm not committing my past to God and until I trust Him with it, how can I expect anyone else to trust me?"

From that day on, though nothing had changed, I felt better about it and didn't throw a pity party on the lawn each time I cut down what I called enemy-number-one with the push mower. But as the ordeal continued for weeks, and the days became stifling hot in July, June grew concerned about her fifty-year-old husband suffering heat stroke.

Despite my hatred for the situation, I reminded her that we had to trust God to answer our prayer in his time, hopefully before winter came, and reassured her I was okay. "Honey, I pray as I push. Besides this is super exercise for a great athlete who hydrates before each game in the Cooper Bowl. "

"Yeah, Super Cooper Bowl Man, I was hoping when dad saw you killing yourself in the heat, that it would soften his heart toward you."

"I'm mowing when I get home from work, so it's not so bad...besides someday our first Adam will be coming out, and he can help me."

June touched my shoulder, "Yeah, someday, but what really bothers me is they ignore you, act like you don't exist, but want me to hang out with them as if nothing was wrong."

But on that very day when we were about to give up on someday, a breakthrough came. It was about ninety-nine degrees with high humidity, but as usual June's father was sitting on the front porch of the apartment looking down over the vast lawn as I mowed. I glanced up at him and the urge hit me to pray for him, so I said, "Father I knew it bothers DG a lot to not be able to get up and down the stairs to go and do for himself...please restore his strength."

The prayer had just left my lips when I pushed past him. To my amazement, for the first time, he motioned down to me, so I stopped in my tracks and turned the mower engine off.

He yelled down to me, "Kind of hot to be pushing a lawn mower isn't it?"

In shock, I stammered, "Y...es, yes, sir." *I don't think he heard me.*

"Well," he said, "why don't you ride that Snapper I got out there in the shed?"

Still in shock, I sort of nodded and said, "That sounds like good advice to me." *I guess I've proven myself to him...in some way..*

I parked my little mower, cranked up his big one and began to mow the field around his place. Dad Marchant was all smiles. After thanking God for hearing our prayer for reconciliation with her father, I prayed for DG again that God would heal him, but it wasn't a prayer of faith because I couldn't concentrate on his health when I was scared to death that I would wreck his mower or ruin the blades on tree roots. *Give me favor, God; I can't blow this now; got to build on the favor he has shown me.* He reminded me of my father and that wasn't necessarily a good thing. My dad was a mechanically inclined workman who could not only operate machinery but figure out what made it work. *He's the opposite of me.* On the next pass by, I waved to him, smiled, but said to myself, *I hope I don't screw up like I always did with Dad. I sure hope I can impress him...oh God please don't let him find out that I'm a nervous wreck worried about wrecking his toy.*

I finished the section nearest his apartment building and moved on to a one acre field west of our home. From his upstairs perch he still had an eagle's eye view of me as I began the work on higher ground. Despite my fear of screwing up, a feeling of pride rose up in me. *I'm riding Dad Marchant's Red Snapper. Man, can this thing cut grass!*

It was a beautiful North Florida afternoon to cut grass on high ground, but a tropical storm had stalled off Atlantic Beach two days before and dropped over two inches during its North Florida vacation. That left the low area land of the property mushy with water. I was too busy enjoying the moment to notice how wet the lower field was. *Red* was cutting through the grass with ease so I would finish in a fraction of the time push-mowing required. Motoring along I envisioned hitting a few practice golf shots off the freshly mown turf after finishing.

Suddenly, Red bogged down to a jolting stop in the muddy terrain. My lips became a thin red line. "Dumb machine," I bellowed, "hope June's dad is not watching now." I turned the blades off. I glanced up toward his house and thanked God he had gone in the house. Then I considered

188

the wetness, left the engine running in first gear and hopped off the seat. That was my first mistake. The engine died.

I didn't know the machine had a safety feature that caused the engine to shut off when no one was on the seat. It took me five minutes to figure that out, crank it up again and keep it running. Once the motor was idling I placed a concrete block on the seat and smiled at my ingenuity. Afraid Mr. Marchant would come back out of the house and see his mower bogged down in the mud, I jumped around behind the machine and pushed with all my might. That was my second sad mistake. The Mean Red Machine wouldn't budge, though the wheels were spinning like crazy and slinging mud all over me. My feet were sinking deeper into the mire, so I kicked off a bit of mud and stepped to the side to assess the situation. It appeared the best plan was to get around in front and pull the big mower out. That was my third sad mistake.

When I grabbed a hold of Red and pulled, he grunted, coughed, and roared out of the bog. I lost my footing and twisted my body as he knocked me face down into the mud. At impact the concrete block toppled off the seat and the engine and mower blades shut down without mowing my legs.

I jumped up and checked things out. There was mud all over me with the mower resting on my lower body, but no blood. My ego was hurt more than my legs. I looked up to the porch once again to see if my father-in-law or anyone else had seen my accident. It appeared no one had. I thanked God for that, washed myself and the machine and put it up as though nothing had happened.

To my surprise, the next day when I shared the caper with my new father-in-law, he laughed with me rather than at me. And somehow in that moment he accepted me as his son-in-law and began to treat me like a son, sharing a tall cool lemon-aid with me when I took a break from mowing what he called "our tree acres of paradise" on Old Red.

29

The following Saturday morning while I was mowing grass again, Mr. Johnson, the executer of the estate of our deceased neighbors who had lived in the house to the east of us for thirty years, approached me.

As he came across the lawn, he smiled, waved his hand toward the field I just mowed and said, "I see you are taking good care of your yard and Mr. Marchant's; I like your style on the mower."

I laughed. "Oh, no, you saw me get stuck in the bog."

He smiled and nodded, "You're pretty quick getting out of the way."

The blood rushed into my face. "You saw me get run over by the mower."

"Yeah, I'm still laughing at that sight, but you're doing a great job taking care of the place...if not yourself."

I laughed again and said, "Machines and I don't mix too well, but I like working outside and improving the home place."

"How would you like to buy this one?" he asked.

"Sold!" I exclaimed.

He looked at me like I was crazy. "Don't you want to know how much?"

I laughed. "Yes, but I know you will be fair, neighbor."

"Tell you what; I'll get it appraised and that will be the sales price." Mr. Johnson promised.

"Sounds fair to me."

We shook hands. When he withdrew his hand, he said, "It surprised me you acted so fast."

"I have been praying about it for months. My father-in-law can't live upstairs anymore, and I asked the Lord to make this little brick house available for them."

"Now, I'm not surprised."

"One thing I want you to know, though, Mr. Johnson, is about my past..."

He held up his hand. "That bank robbing stuff I knew about: most everybody in the neighborhood does, I reckon."

I didn't know what to say.

He continued, "That doesn't bother me, but it sounds like it bothers you."

I smiled. "Yeah, seems like that's the truth."

"I read people well; you're an honest man now."

"Thank you, sir! What a blessing!"

"No, thank *you*. Mainly I wanted someone to have the property that would take good care of it. But please stay on the mower, not under it."

I laughed and laughed, finally collected myself, and said, "Well, I'm going to tell a banker friend about it."

"Who's that?"

"Hugh Jones, president of the Barnett Bank, asked me to come by and see him when I decide to finance something, so I believe he will help me get a mortgage for the property."

My banking business experience, as diverse, perverse and mind boggling as it had been, did not prepare me for the reception I received when I entered the Barnett Tower in downtown Jacksonville. A smartly dressed attractive young woman greeted me when I stepped through the door of the Barnett Bank. "Mr. Cooper, Mr. Jones is expecting you; please follow me," she said without asking me my name, or introducing herself.

"What if my name isn't Cooper?"

"Mr. Jones described you...said you would be punctual, if not five minutes early, and dressed like a gentleman."

That line sent my emotions skyrocketing. *Mr. Jones has told her "The Gentleman Bank Robber" is coming to dine. Now, all I need is for her or him to ask me which Barnett Banks I robbed.*

"Are you okay, sir...sir, are you okay?" I heard someone ask.

I woke up from the daze to realize it was my escort, who had turned and faced me. "Please excuse me, miss; I was taking a trip."

At that moment, when we arrived at the elevator that would take us to the top floor of the building and Mr. Jones' suite of offices, she pushed the control button, turned her head and said, "My name is Donna Downey."

"It's my pleasure to meet you; I am Ken Cooper," I said, as I extended my hand and shook hers.

As we whizzed to the top of the skyscraper, I asked, "Have you been to the top of the new First Union Bank?"

"Well, no sir, I haven't," she said, her hesitant high tone telling me the question surprised her."

It had surprised me, too. My impulse was to share the traumatic experience of a few weeks ago, when I was locked in the building at lunch time, but I didn't. I simply said, "I was there for my lunch break recently."

"I'm sure Mr. Jones will top them," she said, smiled, and added, "Sometimes I believe he thinks this is the Top of the Mark!"

"San Francisco...one of my favorite restaurants," I said.

Miss Downey nodded, the elevator door opened and she escorted me into a lobby full of people, young men and women...*Yuppies who looked just like her*...several of them ogling me. Adrenaline coursed through my body much like it had in bank lobbies before the hold ups, but as I studied them I saw that their eyes were bright and their faces, friendly, their body language non-threatening, but I noted that not one of them stepped forward to meet me. I thought *They know me; they know me...the Gentleman Bank Robber!...why in the world did I accept Mr. Jones' invitation?*

Miss Downey led me through the gauntlet of gawkers without incident and past several offices to Mr. Jones' private restaurant replete with black napkins over white table cloths. I felt out of place and my mind couldn't receive the site before me as I remembered the Time for Christ fundraiser where I met Mr. Jones. *"He's a prince of the people...the prophecy that I would rub elbows with the princes of Jacksonville has come true indeed, or will it be about Moe's prophecy that bankers are out to get me?*

Miss Downey interrupted my mind trip. "Have a seat, Mr. Cooper; Mr. Jones will join you shortly. Would you like a cup of coffee while you wait?" she asked.

"No, no thank you, Ma'am; I'll enjoy the view if I may," I said and stepped toward a huge wrap around window that would provide a breathtaking view of the River City for a former bank robber from the mountains who suddenly felt like a fish out-of-water.

A few seconds after Miss Downey disappeared, I heard Mr. Jones' voice behind me.

"Don't you love this view of downtown Jacksonville?" he asked.

I turned around to greet him, "I'd love to have my office right here overlooking the St. Johns winding its way through the River City," I said.

He laughed and shook my hand. "I don't need another banker just now."

I loved his sense of humor and friendly manner, but I must have sounded formal when I replied, "Mr. Jones, thanks for inviting me to dine with you." I had mouthed the words and rehearsed them since I received the invitation a week earlier.

"You are most welcome; but please call me, Hugh."

"I'll try to, sir, but I'm rather overwhelmed to be here with you." I couldn't bring myself to tell him how deeply his hospitality had affected me and how out-of-place I felt.

"You've got something against good food, Ken?"

"No, Mr. Jones, erh...Hugh, and it hasn't anything to do with banks," I said, lying, in an attempt to lighten my mood and not give way to the tears of gratitude that were welling up and about to spill out of me.

Mr. Jones laughed. "I'm glad you visited us later than sooner," he said with a twinkle in his bright blue eyes and pointed to a table facing the huge window.

Once seated, I began to relax. *I like this man.* After glancing at the menu, I waved toward the magnificent view and said, "Thank you, I love looking at the river winding its way through downtown to the ocean...this is fabulous, and I'll top it off by ordering my favorite...seafood."

Mr. Jones laughed. His laughter was just as real as he was, but his tenor tone became serious. "I want the city to be as good to you as it has been to me," he said as he motioned to an orderly standing nearby. "Mr. Cooper will have the Shrimp Paradiso and please bring me a Reuben sandwich with extra sour kraut on the side."

As expected the food was excellent...fit for a prince. We laughed and talked our way through a delightful meal and I was grateful that Mr. Jones didn't ask me anything about my banking "career" though he did mention it in passing when he said, "I didn't know bank robbers had such good credit."

"What do you mean...you checked my credit?"

He laughed. "Yes, before I asked you to lunch...I figured you needed help getting started again."

My skin tingled and the ever present tears prevented me from looking him in the eyes, but I managed to say, "I'm amazed, sir; I don't know what to say."

"Your excellent credit rating said it for you, Ken."

I laughed. "I have always had good financial credit, now I've got to work on my social credibility."

Mr. Jones ignored the twisted pun, cleared his throat and assumed an exaggerated banker's stance. "The Barnett Mortgage Company considers it an honor to serve you, Mr. Cooper."

"Well, you amaze me, Mr. Jones, but I came hoping that you would consider financing a house for me," I blurted.

"It's a deal!" he declared.

Mr. Jones' declaration robbed me of words and I choked on a bit of shrimp. I cleared my throat and said, "I'm very grateful, sir, but don't you need to know the facts?"

He smiled. "Your neighbor told me you wanted to buy his house, a little red brick home for your in-laws; after lunch I'll walk across the street with you, introduce you to the division manager of the mortgage company and get the facts to get things under way for you."

Though the significance of the moment had not sunk in yet, I was speechless that a banker would reach out and love me, a former bank robber, in an easy, matter-of-fact way that would empower me to ultimately erase the negative self image of a social outcast.

30

With Mr. Jones' backing, financing the little brick house for Mom and Dad Marchant became a "done deal" in a matter of days and they moved in within a month. I felt like a "prince of the people" and my ear-to-ear smile reflected it everywhere I went. I called Moe and told him that not all bankers hated me...that at least one loved me, but I didn't know what would happen a week later, when an entire church congregation rejected my wife and me to fulfill that part of his "prophecy."

Hugh Jones helped me to see that there are forgiving, loving people in society, even bankers, who are eager to help former bank robbers make a clean fresh start. He had suffered through several robberies in his thirty years in banking that injured him and his staffs emotionally, but he loved me and reached out to help me anyway. I was amazed by his grace, but people in church pews helped me to see that, religious or not, a lot of parishioners cannot forgive the criminal much less forget what he has done.

June and I were motivated to attend a small to medium sized church near our home where we could be fed spiritually and grow in our devotion to God and to each other. We felt that my new beginning required that we place ourselves under the authority of a church pastor, who could guide us through the word of God. Though she attended a Catholic church as a youth, June had given her life to Christ in a Baptist church when she was a mere lass of twelve. And at the age of fifteen she became a founding member of *Broward Road Baptist Church*, a small local congregation about a mile from our home.

The Sunday after we closed on the house for Dad and Mom Marchant, though June had not been there for years, we visited the neighborhood church, thinking that it might be God's place for us, but were we ever in for a surprise! From the moment we walked into the huge sanctuary with a scattering of about eighty people in attendance, until we left, not one person spoke to us or even acknowledged our presence.

Following the service, as we drove away toward El Potro's, our favorite Mexican Food restaurant, for lunch, I teased June about her being a founding member. "It seems to me that the people of Broward Road Church should at least raise their heads, look into your bright eyes and say, 'Hi'...even though they ignore your bank robber-husband."

"I can't believe that happened, Ken...I'm in shock...surely, it had nothing to do with you; if you had tried to take up a collection at gun point, I could see it, but..."

I interrupted her with laughter. "Well, maybe it's because they're like some of the church members who don't know how to respond to strangers."

"I don't think that's it at all, honey. It seemed to me that they were so much into themselves that they didn't notice us...though we were seated on an aisle near the middle of the church."

We laughed about it, prayed and returned the next week to worship. To our amazement, the same thing happened: not one person spoke to us or acknowledged our presence even when the regulars walked among the pews greeting each other. Back home over lunch, though befuddled and frustrated, we tried to discuss the situation objectively to determine why we were ignored and rejected by the church people.

June touched my hand. "Some of those people recognized me...they were not rejecting you...they were rejecting me and the boys as well."

I figured June was referring to the fact that one of her sons was in prison for the accidental shooting death of his brother, but instead of delving into an emotionally loaded subject I resorted to humor, saying, "Because they remember you from several years ago as a boot stompin', mini skirted member of the Harper Valley PTA."

June laughed with me, and the laughter seemed to begin to heal us. By the end of our discussion we agreed to continue talking to God about the matter rather than discussing it with other people.

Morning after morning, and as we passed the church during the day, June and I prayed that God would help us forgive the people and asked him to lead us to a church home, preferably a Baptist congregation because of our early roots in that kind of church. We also asked him to send us to a small- to medium-sized congregation that had a heart for prison ministry and some semblance of understanding of prisoners and their needs as they come out of prison.

The next five churches received us with open arms, but we still had difficulty finding a spiritual home. Though we favored a Baptist church, the challenge of choosing a place to worship stemmed from my beginning days as a Christian in prison. At Union Correctional at Raiford where all the colors of the Christian Rainbow met in the chapel to worship, I blended in with all the hues and tints of believers and had no denominational preference. So for Sundays on end, I dragged June through the alphabet...from the Assemblies of God to three different kinds of Baptist congregations to a traditional Catholic church, a charismatic Catholic, to several stripes of Episcopalian, and Lutheran, along with the Methodist and Presbyterian congregations, not to mention those assemblies who named their church after a road or street but called themselves interdenominational or "community." In a matter of ten months we visited more than thirty churches in Jacksonville. Except for the ones whose members could not love an ex-offender enough to picture June and me as members of their congregation, I loved them all. In fact the more I learned about each congregation, their mission visions-- especially those involved in the Kairos Prison Ministry -- the more I loved them, and the more confused and ambivalent I became when trying to choose one over another.

Finally, after months of floundering, God sent a man, a second Mister Jones, to rescue me. Like Hugh, his unrelated "cousin", Dan Jones understood my coal camp ways and accepted me despite my criminal history. He called himself a hillbilly from the coal camps of West Virginia. From the moment I met him at the North Side Business Men's Club I related to him and trusted Dan to help me find a home church.

31

It turned out to be North Jacksonville Baptist Church, where Dan, his wife, Sandra, and his family attended. On a bright North Florida autumn Sunday morning they took us to a worship service. Our first impression was positive despite the size of the building and congregation. Second in magnitude only to the First Baptist Church in downtown Jacksonville, a monstrous building that seated eight thousand worshippers, North Jax, as Dan called it, seated more than four thousand.

From the first song, we enjoyed the hundred voice choir, but we were overjoyed with the preaching. Pastor Harold Hunter delivered a well documented, dynamic, soul searching message on the power of the tongue from the Third Chapter of the Book of James and he wore cowboy boots as he strode back and forth across the stage. I nudged June and said, "I like it here, babe...the music, the word of God from a down-home cowboy preacher...perfect."

June squeezed my hand and said, "I do too; let's come back."

After our third visit we became members, and a few weeks later, Dan asked me to accompany him to his Sunday School class.

As Dan and I approached the class room, my hands became wet with sweat as I relived the Sunday school scene with the Watters boy at Mother's church in Kentucky. Dan touched me on the shoulder and told me he was the teacher and I was the guest speaker.

I stopped in my tracks and said, "Doggone it, Hillbilly, I wouldn't have agreed to do this if you'd told me that."

"I know, Ninety-nine, that's the reason I didn't."

Wrinkles formed on my forehead when he called me by my old prison nickname so I asked, "How are you going to introduce me?" He didn't answer me, but laughed a loud guttural guffaw like only men from the coal mine hollers can *holler* ...a deep and extended gurgle from out of his belly that back in the coal country would have projected the sound from one mountain top to the next. I lagged behind him as he continued marching toward the classroom, so he turned, came back to me, put his hand on my shoulder, peered down into my eyes and declared, "To save confusion and questions later on, I'm going to introduce you the way people think of you."

"That's what I'm afraid of...just like you introduce me to business groups before I speak: My friend, the bank robber."

"Exactly...I'll say something like this: 'Fellows, this is Ken Cooper; you've probably seen his byline on newspaper articles...he's a staff writer for the Times-Union newspaper, wrote an article titled Moses Moves the People to the Promised Land, when we finished the church and relocated here on north Main Street. I'm proud of that, but I'm prouder to introduce you to my friend in Christ, a Gentleman Bank Robber Blessed by God.'"

I stopped and whined, "That's what I'm afraid of. You could at least say former."

Dan guffawed again and dragged me toward his classroom. When I passed through the door I wanted to pass out. The knot in my stomach told me I was about to face the same gut wrenching I suffered when I joined a circle of men at mom's church. But as I gazed into the faces of the men circled up, I said to myself, *These guys look different...soft eyes, pleasant, happy faces...they can't "see" the prison number stamped on my forehead.*

At that moment, Dan woke me up: "Fellows, meet our guest speaker, this is Ken Cooper, the Gentleman Bank Robber." Though he had presented me in that way when he introduced me to speak at civic groups, it handcuffed me but apparently set the class free. A tall man seated to Dan's left laughed and with a loud voice like Dan's said, "Welcome, Ken, at least we know about you...Dan hides behind his real estate license... to steal."

A roar of laughter filled the room. Before Dan could respond to the hilarious barb, a sharp dressed handsome man in his early thirties, stood up, shook my hand and said, "There's three or four other crooks in here...*we* just haven't been caught." The group roared again. *I think he meant it!*

From that moment on, I felt at home and following the worship time, June and I went out to lunch with Dan and Sandra.

Seated at a table for four at Joseph's Italian Restaurant on Main Street, a mile south of the church, I teased June about what motivated me to join the church. "Where can you find a spirit-filled pastor like Harold Hunter who preaches the Word of God in manure-kicking cowboy boots?"

204

"Nowhere but in Texas," Dan said as we all laughed.

"Seriously," June broke in, "he's the one you need to talk to about going into full-time ministry."

In an attempt to skirt the subject June had introduced, I ignored her statement and said, "I hate cowboy boots...they cramp my toes...and my spiritual style."

Dan grabbed my arm and a cloud came over his face. "You're not thinking about leaving the paper, are you?"

"Yes, we have been praying about it for some time," I said.

"What would you do?" Sandra asked as she looked at June.

"We would do prison ministry...you know, *Adopt a Man* coming out of prison to a half way house, and preaching in jails and prisons," June said as she reached across the table and touched my arm.

Hair on my neck became electric, so to short circuit the conversation, I said, "Uh, really, writing for the Times-Union is something of a ministry when I write about Christians."

Dan nodded and said, "I kept the story you wrote about North Jax moving from Pearl Street across the Trout River to the 'Promised Land.'"

We laughed "Yeah, the Lord and pastor Harold Hunter forgave me for likening him to Moses in cowboy boots."

"Look out, 'Preacher Boy,' you'll have to face Moses when you cross the Jordan," Dan said.

"Yeah, and speaking of the Jordan, it may be a kind of death to leave my job."

Dan and Sandra looked puzzled.

June noticed and said "Tell them the latest bad news, Ken."

I downed a hard swallow of water and said, "Jim Whyte...uh, the editorial staff assigned me to the news room."

"That sounds like good news to me?" Dan said.

I smiled ruefully. "It would be for some writers who like to write straight news stories...not features like the Promised Land story."

Dan nodded his head and Sandra broke in, "That's not as much fun, is it?"

I placed my hands on the table "No...it's not *me*... I really enjoy writing features about people, human interest stuff ...what makes them tick... like Bob Murray, your evangelist buddy from Missouri... your article about his travels in a dilapidated old flivver all over the state of Georgia where he now lives."

"Yeah that was fun; Bob did quite a few years in prison, now he's busy traveling as an evangelist...hey, I've got an idea."

"Tell me; tell me!"

"Why don't you talk to Pastor Harold first, get his guidance and blessing, and then talk to Bob about his experience in a full-time faith ministry," Dan suggested.

I laughed. "Last week I met with Pastor Hunter, and he told me it's hard to kick against the prodding of the Lord when he's calling you out into ministry."

"What else did he say?"

"He told me if God was for me, no man could come against God's plan."

"He's right, of course." Dan said and then added, "But you had better know that it is his plan and calling."

June interrupted our dialogue: "I have peace about Ken going into fulltime ministry, but I would like for him to talk to Bob Murray first."

Responding to June, I said, "I will; he's the perfect one to talk to me about an ex-convict going into fulltime ministry. Though he has been out only two years he is doing really well as a prison evangelist."

Dan said, "Amen," and added, "Our Brother Bob preaches to sinners in church pews... and in prisons."

We all laughed, and I said. "He's stopping by next week. Bob can help me sort through things... maybe help me find peace that the Lord really could use me in fulltime ministry."

32

The following Thursday morning Bob Murray and I walked and talked on a stretch of beach about twenty miles from our home. Ten minutes into the stroll the sun peeked over the Atlantic, spread golden rays across the shimmering water and cast long shadows of two *giants,* one skinny and one stout, as we sauntered along the sandy shore from Big Talbot Island State Park toward Amelia Island, ten miles to the north. The longer we talked the shorter our shadows became. The warm sun on our right, the cool ocean breeze swirling behind us...the sandy beach was a perfect place for a long talk about a serious matter.

Like angels in disguise, from time to time, sea gulls flying overhead dipped down the way they do in Florida prisons along the ocean and gulf to eavesdrop, beg for food and squawk to us that they knew about freedom in a world that really didn't understand them and hardly tolerated them.

I motioned toward our heavenly visitors, but looked down into the two shadows that followed us and thought about Bob's criminal past. He trained Kentucky race horses in the Bluegrass State where he drew fraud charges for selling a "shadow" of a thoroughbred to a prominent family back in his home state of Missouri... amazing that a worthless grandson of a priceless stud horse could be passed off as the real deal.

My beach buddy must have read my mind. He stopped dead in his tracks, turned and pointed down to his shadow that now appeared as wide as it was high. He said, "Too bad we can't sell a shadow of me, as valuable as I am."

I shrieked and motioned toward my shadow, "Yeah, yours would bring a lot more than this skinny race horse."

Bob became serious: "Ninety-nine, my rebellion turned five years for fraud into twenty-five for assault and battery on guards!"

To change the course of our conversation from dark memories to the present, I cupped my hand into a "microphone" and mouthed an imaginary news headline: "Former prisoner turns preacher man!"

Bob pointed down at our feet and declared, "The Lord gives ugly thieves beautiful feet and sets them free to follow Him."

"Amen!" I said, adding, "Into ministry."

Bob leaped into the air and threw his hands toward the sea birds above us. "Like them, I preach freedom every day!"

I laughed, raced toward a noisy wave crashing on the beach, and yelled, "I'm free! I'm free!"

Bob pointed to the ocean and said, "Ken, though you did only three years on ninety-nine, I'm sure freedom is just as sweet to you."

I extended my arms as if to embrace the ocean. "It's as big and wide as the Atlantic; I can't get enough of freedom...whatever it is," I said, laughing.

Bob glanced at me, eased away from the water, but rather than walking further, he sat on a sand hill graced by sea oats dancing in the ocean breeze. I followed him and sat down facing the ocean. He held my eyes with his and said, "Listen, lame duck, before we return to the car so you can go to work, let's pray about your future."

Hearing Bob's tilted reference to my leaving the newspaper, I dabbed a tear and nodded my approval.

But instead of praying, my evangelist friend continued talking: "Remember how the Kairos Prison Ministry people taught us to talk to God about a man before we talked to the man about God."

I opened my eyes and beat my chest. "That's one of my favorite sayings, and I'm ready to talk to God about this man."

My big brother in Christ simply raised his head toward heaven and said, "Dear heavenly Father, I thank you for Brother Ken and your plans for his future. Amen!"

Sorely disappointed that Bob hadn't prayed earnestly about God giving me peace about leaving the newspaper to pursue prison ministry, I wanted to stay put, but he got up and began the long walk required to return to our cars. As usual I followed him. On the way Bob broke out into a tune that lifted my spirits and let me know that my ex-convict mentor approved of my desire to follow his example in preaching God's word: "How beautiful upon the mountain are the feet of those who preach glad tidings of good news."

33

Two days later, Raymond Duncan and his wife, Lynda, confirmed God's message. They invited June and me to dine with them at the Sawgrass Marriott Hotel and Resort at Ponte Vedra Beach located some thirty miles south of Jacksonville, but only a three iron shot from the TPC Sawgrass where the world's elite golfers gathered once a year for The Players Championship. As the four of us arrived at the magnificent hotel that commands a tropical overlook near the Atlantic, I forgot about trying to figure out God's plan for ministry. I felt like a world champion golfer in paradise. Stepping out of the car to enter the resort I looked at June and said, "When you married me, you made me the champion of the world."

She blushed, glanced at Lynda and said, "Don't knock yourself out, champ; I know what championship you're thinking about…"

"Golf is God's calling," Raymond said, laughing as he eased out of the car to speak to the parking valet.

"Doggone it; am I that easy to read?" I asked.

"Much easier than the greens at Sawgrass," Lynda chimed in.

We all laughed and strolled into the Marriott.

In the lobby, while we were waiting for the maître-de, I glanced around and said, "Wouldn't it be great to meet some of my champions."

"Yes, several of the young stars live right here: Jim Furyk, Fred Funk, David Duval, and Vijay Singh," Raymond enthused.

"My, oh my, would I ever love to play the famous island green on the seventeenth hole with them!"

"I wonder if you'd make a hole in one?" June asked, smiling.

"Dream on, honey."

"You wouldn't have a prayer of even hitting that small green, especially with the pros at your elbows," Lynda said.

"Speaking of elbows, Ken," Raymond broke in, adding, "I'd like to take you to a close knit prayer circle that meets at a friend's house next Tuesday."

"If it's to pray that I would have more time to play golf, I'll go."

Lynda touched my hand and said, "Seriously, you will enjoy Jack and Veronica Conover."

The Tuesday night prayer meeting at the Conover's home was more than I bargained for. As Raymond promised, we sat in an elbow-to-elbow circle of eight, but when each of us introduced ourselves to the group, the woman to my immediate left gave her name as Susan Jasper and said she worked for First Union Bank as a counselor for bank robbery victims. I wanted to die right there, looked across the circle toward Raymond, who was seated next to Jack Conover. I caught my friend's eye to see if he had set this up to "help" me. His upraised eyebrows and scrunched shoulders told me he was as surprised as I was. Things got worse.

When the next lady introduced herself, she said that she came because she'd heard that Ms. Jasper would be there to pray for people like her who were suffering from bank robbery trauma. At that point, in a sense, I did die. My mind left my body, bolted out the front door and didn't return until the person on my right nudged me with his elbow and asked me if I were okay. I intoned, "No, I'm not, but I can't talk about it."

Mr. Conover cleared his throat to let us know cross conversations were not allowed in the group. Then he made eye contact with his large gentle brown eyes and told me it was my turn to give my name, occupation and why I came to the meeting. I swallowed hard, cleared my throat and said, "I can't believe what I'm about to say...I really can't do it, uh, uh, I'm Ken Cooper, a staff writer at the Florida Times-Union."

"What's so bad about that?" Jack asked, laughing.

The circle broke into an uproar and laughed until I held up my hands. "I'm going to tell you...maybe because I have a need to tell you, but I'm telling you... I'm a former bank robber."

The crowd broke into more laughter. The look on their faces told me my hosts and their guests thought that I was joking.

Veronica tried to rescue me: "Ken is serious."

A silence as heavy and electric as the air during a bank robbery settled over us.

I broke the silence. "I don't know what to say, except I'm sorry."

More silence. Finally Jack said, "Honestly, Ken, Veronica and I didn't set this up...this is not a confrontation group..."

I looked at Raymond, who remained silent, shrugged my shoulders but no words would come.

"God set it up for me, probably," said the lady who had indicated she was a robber's victim. As she choked out her words she blew her nose with a hanky.

Again, I wanted to die...or run.

The counselor lady to my left touched my arm with her warm hand before she turned, leaned the other direction, and hugged the robbery victim.

Then she placed her hand on my arm, looked at our hostess and said, "Veronica, perhaps this is happening for all of us...but for different reasons for each."

Veronica rose up, walked over to Susan who was still weeping and embraced her.

I wanted to reach out to her, but I was afraid to.

Jack must have read my body language; he eyed me and shook his head "No!"

I was glad but something inside stirred up a desire to do something...anything.

Jack stood up, made his way over to me and like a father, took me into his arms.

Nobody said a word.

A big sigh came out of me and somehow I knew things were going to be okay.

But they weren't.

Susan moved toward me and motioned with her hands for me to stand up.

I did.

214

She put her arms around me and hugged me so tight...and long that my face flushed. It reminded me of my reaction to a banker who hugged me at a Kairos meeting in prison. And the result was similar. Susan and I were in our own little world, and I felt cleaned up and changed from the inside out. A new kind of inner-outer peace came over me that wanted to shout, but I whispered, "I'm free; I'm free!"

"Susan; uh...actually, I didn't rob a bank where you were working, but I really don't deserve to be hugged like this."

She laughed and let go. "I'm not doing it for you; it's for me...I forgive you and him."

"What do you mean him?"

She looked up into my face, laughed and cried at the same time. "I'll be able to feel safe at work again."

"I'm not the only bank robber; I'm so sorry, so sorry," I said, and added, "I pray it will never happen to you again."

Tears of grace welled up, but she didn't say anything.

So, I continued, "You'll be more relaxed now at work and I'll be more relaxed with bank tellers and banks."

Everyone laughed and the meeting ended with a crescendo of joy and a heartfelt peace and feeling of freedom that continued to resonate in my being throughout the week and prepared me for the next close encounter with God as he prepared me for ministry.

34

The following Tuesday at a noon luncheon of the Lion's Club of Jacksonville, the Lord showed up in an unusual way right in the middle of my speech titled, "Publicity, Promotion and the Printed Page." The audience of affluent, dignified movers and shakers of Jacksonville latched on to every word as I shared ideas how they could effectively promote and develop their club through brochures, newspapers and magazines.

Since I was so nervous my knees were knocking I began the presentation by quoting my favorite saying of America's first newspaperman, Ben Franklin, that I memorized and rehearsed with my newspaper boss, Jim Whyte, who set up the speaking engagement.

But before I spoke I stood silent and looked about the audience, made eye contact with several of the bright-eyed people, raised my hands for effect and declared, "If you would not be soon forgotten, when you are dead and rotten, either write things worth the reading or do things worth the writing."

The feedback from the crowd let me know they had not only received the opening punch line but enjoyed it. They leaned forward and nodded at me, or glanced at the person beside them and expressed their approval to them.

The nervous knees stopped quaking and I continued with a bit of boldness, saying, "I am here today because you are doing things worth the writing; you are doing things worth the reading...you are doing community betterment projects worth the planning it takes to effectively promote them."

At that moment, when I paused to let the audience process and meditate on the statement, the crowd erupted in applause. I felt my face flush with excitement and joy juice flowed through my body. I grabbed a copy of that day's Times-Union and held it up to illustrate a point about newspaper promotion. But as I said, "There are thousands of people ready willing and able to support your causes when you let them in on what you are doing and invite them..." I found it difficult to continue to speak as my throat became constricted. I paused, gulped some water, swallowed hard, tried to clear my throat to resume speaking but the words didn't want to come out. I apologized to give myself time to recover. I recognized from past experience that this had happened when the Lord wanted me to change the subject and take a new direction. *Lord, please don't do this weird thing; it's so embarrassing!* I said to myself.

The same thing had occurred several months earlier during a speech to a group of bankers and tellers when in the middle of my talk I abruptly changed the subject and asked the audience of some 500 bankers and 200 tellers to forgive me for robbing their banks. The emotional explosion that occurred convinced me that although the result seemed positive overall, it was a gut-wrenching exasperating experience I didn't want to repeat.

But at the Downtown Lion's Club, when the choking in the throat continued to constrict the word flow, I figured it was definitely God's doing. To gather myself, I paused

217

again, gripped the newspaper in my hand, took another drink of water, and coughed to clear my throat. The audience became restless and my host, the honorable Mrs. Jacqueline Jacobson, the president of the club, raised her hands to her throat in a gesture intended to ask me if I were okay. I nodded that I was, but when I resumed speaking, the choking became so intense I stopped speaking altogether, stepped around the podium and faced the audience. "As you can see, there's a choking in my throat; I don't know if you have ever experienced anything like this, but it happens to me when I'm supposed to change directions in a talk."

A nervous air settled over the audience, some of the listeners coughed, and Mrs. Jacobson shuffled in her seat. I continued, "I hope you'll bear with me...but apparently I must tell you about myself before I go any further."

The atmosphere became heavier so I stammered when I said, "It...it...it's true that I write for the Florida Times-Union, and it's true that ten years ago I was director of publicity for a Christian college in Kentucky, and also served as advertising and tourism promotion director for the great Commonwealth of Kentucky, but it is also true that during those days and beyond in the Bluegrass State that I functioned as a serial criminal.

The faces of the dumbfounded people in the audience turned as white as the newspaper I was holding in my hand and I heard gasping sounds throughout the crowd. Though I wanted to die, somehow I continued, "I have no idea why I'm telling you this, except it bothers me that you may see me as a certain kind of person, perhaps a person like you of high moral character, but I feel like you deserve to know the truth about me.

My flabbergasted audience shuffled in their seats. In attempt to relieve their shock, I said, "With your permission, with your permission..."

Mrs. Jacobson rescued me by saying, "Mr. Cooper, please go ahead."

I glanced at her for a moment, turned back to the crowd that now looked agitated and grim, and said, "Through thirteen years of the robberies, quite a few newspapers wrote articles about a mysterious gentleman bank robber who was certainly not doing things worth the writing. Though the publicity and promotion work I performed flourished during my illicit banking career, I lived a double life...allowed the craving for an adrenaline rush to take over once in a while...I'd plan another holdup and do it."

A lady on the front row swooned; I dropped the crumpled newspaper and blurted; "I was living a double life, split right down the middle. Mr. Nice to everybody most of the time, but on occasion, I would give in to the thirst for the adrenaline juice, and assume my position on the stage, in a bank lobby, where I would experience another adrenaline high from the A-charge that would course through my body and make me feel like Superman or Batman."

Ms. Jacobson stood up, teetered in place, and sat back down. I continued, "So, I guess what I want to say today is that I'm sorry and will you please forgive me?"

The crowd moaned; my host steadied herself and said, "Pray tell, forgive you for what, Mr. Cooper?"

"For robbing those banks, and not being up front with you..."

"You didn't deceive us, and as far as I know you didn't take any of my money," she said.

The Lions roared.

I felt faint but managed a smile, saying, "I hope not...no, but I loathe myself just as much as if you had been a victim I assaulted."

Ms. Jacobson attempted to set me free with a leading question: "Mr. Cooper, please, before you go, will you give us a parting word?"

Hearing her words perked me up but didn't give me a clue as to what my *parting word* should be, but then a quotation I had penned while in the depths of despair in prison flashed before me. Unaware that it could come across as a plea for acquittal or absolution, I held up my hands to the audience and said, "To conjure up some hope, one lonely night in a pit of despair, I grabbed a stub of a pencil and wrote, 'Each day's doing, not yesterday's dark deeds defines one's destiny.'"

There was no applause, no response but bowed heads and eyes that refused to look at me. Once again I wanted to die.

To rescue me for the third and final time, Mrs. Jacobson walked over, hugged me like a reluctant date and sent me away after asking me if I would return at some point and complete the "magnificent talk on how we can promote our club more effectively."

The stunned audience sat in limbo, so I rushed off the stage and escaped in my getaway car, feeling like a total failure and frustrated that I had made a fool of myself, Mrs. Jacobson, and perhaps worse yet, Mr. Whyte.

On the way back to the newspaper office, my mind was so befuddled that I lost my bearings and got off course twice. When I did my return to my desk and computer, I could not focus on writing and sat there mumbling to myself, *I'll gather my stuff up 'cause the axe is sure to fall.* But nothing happened the rest of the wasted day as I "hid" in my computer where I retreated into myself to figure out what was happening within my psyche that caused the irresistible urge to confess my crimes in public. In a sarcastic tone I ridiculed myself and mumbled, "It's an obvious attempt to lose my mind and my job."

35

All day Friday twin demons of paranoia and fear choked me, but then, as I left the building to go home, for no apparent reason they let go and I could breathe again.

But on Monday morning, when the word came down that Mr. Whyte wanted to see me in his office, a cloud of fear engulfed my mind and I had to drag my body into the elevator. Between the first and sixth floors I talked to myself. *Jim never calls me into his office; my shenanigans at the Lion's Club has cooked my goose. I'm as good as gone. I'm a goner. Fired and unemployed. What can I tell June? This cannot be good news.*

But it was, and the good news came in the person of Mrs. Jacobson from the Lion's Club, who rose to greet me with a warm handshake when I entered Mr. Whyte's office. The glow on her face and the twinkle in her eyes baffled me and the words that came out of her mouth sent me reeling. "I stopped by to congratulate Mr. Whyte on his wisdom in hiring a good man like you, Mr. Ken Cooper."

I stood speechless...and felt foolish.

She continued, "I was just telling Jim about the life-changing impact you had on our club members last week."

Though I could hear what she was saying, her words made no sense.

Mrs. Jacobson smiled and added, "What you didn't know, sir, was that our club was split right down the middle...lots of animosity and hurt feelings on both sides – we weren't communicating - but your words on living a double life and forgiveness opened us up."

"I'm amazed, Mrs. Jacobson; I was simply apologizing for my insane crimes."

"I recognize that, but your caring enough about us to apologize sent a strong message that we needed to do something to bridge the gap between ourselves."

"I'm not sure I understand," I said as I glanced at my boss.

She said, "After the meeting, we stayed around and shared our true feelings...positive and negative...in a humble spirit."

I looked at Mr. Whyte, but said to her, "That's always helpful."

"Yes, it was and led to our forgiving each other."

"I'm amazed," I said.

"So were we and I came today to thank you and let you know we want you to come back and finish your talk."

I looked at Jim and said, "If Mr. Whyte allows me to."

She smirked, "I'll guarantee he will, but you must guarantee me you will use the same quote that helped open our hearts and eyes."

Jim and I laughed, looked at each other, opened our mouths and in unison declared, "If you would not be soon forgotten when you are dead and rotten, either write things worth the reading or do things worth the writing."

Mrs. Jacobson showed her delight by applauding, but she said, "That's a good one but not the one...the one I was talking about was the saying you wrote in prison about your destiny."

Tears filled my eyes. I took out a handkerchief, blew my nose and said, "Give me a minute....I did that writing in a time of deep despair and hopelessness."

My new ally held back tears, looked at Jim and said, "Take your time."

Jim blew his nose and nodded to approve.

I slipped my hanky back into a pocket and said, "Each day's doing, not yesterday's dark deeds defines one's destiny."

"That's it!" She shouted as she rose up to hug me. This time she embraced me like my Aunt Dessie: warmly, reassuringly.

I didn't know what to say and remained silent. Mr. Whyte stood up, laughed and said. "If you don't finish your speech next time you'll have to answer to this lion."

Ms. Jacobson and I joined him in laugher.

"But then," she said, "You need to get him out in the community speaking more, sir!"

Jim said that he would and when Ms. Jacobson left the office, he congratulated me for a fine job, but with tongue in cheek, he asked, "Ken, does that mean that you control your own destiny?"

Rather than answering his rhetorical question, I said, "Wow, Jim, that takes me back to prison where we played games with Ben Franklin sayings...and you beat me every time."

He laughed. "Let's do it again some time. That was lots of fun, but back to work with you now, my boy!"

"Please, boss, just a moment to tell you about my good deeds that are in the doing now."

"Well, if your Lion's Club speech is any indication, God is pleased with what you are doing, my friend!"

"I hope so and I'm going to jail with volunteers, George Turner and Fred Young, two local evangelists... and expect to preach in the prisons as the Lord opens the doors."

"One thing for sure, your testimony packs a lot of hope for people of all kinds...but frankly, I'm surprised with what happened at the Lion's Club."

"I am, too, sir!"

Jim laughed. "You may be even more surprised by Ms. Simmons if you don't get back to work."

"Thanks for talking to me, Jim; I'm going, I'm going."

He followed me to the door and said, "Ms. Simmons says you are doing a good job with the *Neighbor*, writing and serving as editor of the *Northside Neighbor* edition."

"I wish I could type as fast as I think...like you...but I'm especially happy when I do human interest stories."

"Well, off with you as fast as you can type...your real boss may fire us both."

All the way back to my computer I thanked God for his favor: *Father, God, thank you, thank you, thank you, for Mrs. Jacobson coming into my life, but especially for bringing Jim Whyte into prison to meet me...helping me get out early, and now providing me with one of the best jobs in Jacksonville. And please help me find the guts to talk to Jim about leaving the newspaper to do fulltime speaking ministry.*

The following Tuesday Bob Murray returned to town so we could talk about organizing and developing a faith-based ministry. But he drove up in a major distraction, a brand new Cadillac that I knew nothing about. As we walked and talked on the sandy shores of the Atlantic, the moment could not have been better. The salt air seemed to open up our pipes and minds as we shared our thoughts until our skin looked as red as a Georgia peach. Though we intended to talk about ministry, the main topic for the first three miles was the difficulty he had getting used to a fast-paced world he left behind twenty-five years earlier. "I've danced through these first few months of freedom like a high-strung Kentucky racehorse breaking from the starting gate, Ken."

Responding in his language, I laughed and said, "I guess mine has been a trot since I came out a year ago, but on a mud track from time to time."

Bob smiled, took off his shoes and socks and waded into the knee deep waves. He turned to me, laughed, and said, "I've got a surprise waiting for you back in the parking lot."

"You're glowing like the morning sun; what's up?"

"You'll see...you heard my testimony a couple of weeks ago in Ocala. I am traveling as an evangelist, unbelievable, out only six months from twenty-five years in hell and traveling with a bevy of angels in style."

I focused on the word *evangelist*, rather than his reference to *traveling in style*, and said, "I'd like to try deep water like that."

Bob laughed. "You didn't get my drift, so come on, wade on in, little brother."

I stayed put, scooped a handful of salty brine and flung it into the sea that churned out one boisterous wave after another. "Obviously, you rode back to Jacksonville on waves of joy."

Bob laughed. ""You finally got it, Coop!"

Still thinking of myself and not really listening to him, I played with the valuables in my pockets that would be damaged by the water, lifted my feet to keep them from sinking any further into the ocean ooze and shouted. "John the Baptist wasn't carrying his day-timer and wallet in his back pocket when he baptized people."

Bob laughed and once more attempted to give me a hint about the surprise he had waiting for me back in the parking lot. "Wonder if he had a license to baptize?"

I didn't get it so Bob took another approach. When he stooped down to put his shoes and socks back on he glanced up at me, pointed to the rushing waves and said, "I'm glad you mentioned a driver's license. Can you believe my pastor gave me a brand new car...a Cadillac?"

"You're crazy," I said laughing.

Bob joined me and said, "So nobody won't have to chauffeur me around telling people about Jesus."

"You shouldn't be lying like this, Bob."

Bob beamed. "Thanks again for the newspaper article about my needing a car to travel in."

"You're welcome, but why are you kidding me?"

Bob laughed. "It's a brand spanking new one parked back in the parking lot...I've tried to tell you about it for ten minutes."

"You're serious!" I shouted. "Amazing, I still find it hard to believe...no strings attached, a new Cadillac worth a year's wage...wow!"

"Yes, I'm serious, pastor Mac gave me, an ex-convict evangelist, a ride worth more than he makes."

I gave Bob a hug and in our excitement the *little boys in us* took over and we ran and probably skipped all the way back to area where Bob had parked his Cadillac. Was I ever in for a pleasant surprise!

36

It was even more spectacular than I had envisioned, a top-of-the-line golden El Dorado fit for a king, but given to a *King's kid*. As we walked around it and sat in the plush leather seats that smelled factory new, Bob touched my hand and said, "Ken, I want you to say a prayer to dedicate Nathaniel...that's what I've named him...so he will always be true and used for God's glory."

I said I would, but asked, "Before I pray, if you can, talk to me about the meaning of the name, Nathaniel."

Bob burst out in laughter and said, Nathaniel means "A man of God with no guile."

"Wow! That's perfect! A friend in prison named Nathaniel was exactly that to me."

"Pastor Mac preached on Nathaniel last Sunday, the very day he gave me the car."

"Praise the Lord, I said. We eased out of the car and stepped around to the front of it. I placed my hand on the Cadillac emblem and prayed, "Father, this vehicle has been dubbed Nathaniel so we dedicate him as a spotless gift from you to all those who hear the story of how you met the ministry needs of Bob through his pastor. May Nathaniel help them trust you to meet their needs. We pray this in the name of Jesus. Amen."

Shortly after that Bob drove away in Nathaniel, leaving me gazing at the sea and thanking God for his goodness. As I watched the breakers crash on he shore, I wondered how God would meet our needs once June and I launched a ministry. I had no idea that pastor Mac would call me two months later to tell me some very disconcerting news about Nathaniel.

When I picked up the phone in my office, he practically shouted in my ear: "Ken you'll never believe what your crazy friend did!"

"Tell me please, is Bob okay?"

"Yes, he's fine, but I'm not!"

"What in the world is going on?"

"He gave Nathaniel to a pastor down state!."

Astonishment clouded my senses for a moment, but then I recovered to say, "Sounds just like Bob...I've seen him give people his shoes, clothing, whatever they'd ask him for...but not his beloved Nathaniel."

"Well he did it, and I'm going – Ken, there's another line. I've got to go, but, well, let me put it this way: I'll never give him another one!"

"No," I said, laughing before he hung up, "You ought to insist on that."

When I cradled the phone, I laughed like a mad man, and in between gasps for air, praised God for Bob Murray and asked Him to help me have the faith to be *crazy* like Bob. I leaned back in my chair, thanked God for my friend and asked him to give Bob another car to drive. And as I sat there a new feeling came over me. Somehow, the favor God showed Bob through his pastor spurred something in me that helped me believe that the Lord would also give me what I needed when June and I went into fulltime ministry. I thought to myself: *It's like Pastor Harold preached last month when I met with him: when God is for you no one can be against you.* I smiled at that truth, grabbed the brown Testament that had been my companion throughout prison, asked God to lead me to the passage he wanted me to meditate on, and almost immediately turned to Romans 8:28 which read: "And we know that all things work together for good to them that love God, to them who are the called according to his purpose."

I closed the little book, meditated on the truth of God's word and prayed, "I know you will take care of June and me...it's your will for us to do the Adam ministry, but on the human side, that means it's time for me to leave the newspaper... that means I must have the approval and blessing of Jim Whyte, who has invested so much in me I can't allow him to feel like I've let him down. In the name of Jesus, Amen!"

When I opened my eyes it was clear to me what I should do. *Like Bob, Jim loves the beach so this will be a perfect place to talk to him about God's plan for me.*

231

37

Though he was from Michigan originally, my mentor attended Miami University's School of Journalism and worked for the Miami Herald for ten years. He definitely had sand in his shoes and loved the beach almost as much as I loved the mountains where I was born. In a playful mood, as we began our stroll along the Atlantic, he addressed me as Coop, his way of teasing me about one of my nicknames in prison.

"Coop," he said as we walked barefooted through the sand that separated his condo on Jacksonville Beach from the ocean, "I'll never forget your first day out of prison...three years ago, chasing waves on this very sand for hours."

"I never caught a one, Jim, but it's right up there among the most defining moments of my life."

He stopped in his tracks and looked at me with an exaggerated quizzical look that only a newspaper chief can conjure up when reading between the lines of a bogus editorial. "What in the world is your headline for that piece of work, Ken?"

"Bank Robber turned minister leaves Times-Union..."

My boss laughed an empty kind of laugh as he led me into the turbulent waves, turned and said, "You're wading into the deep water of ministry already, huh?"

I turned to face him and asked, "You aren't surprised, are you?"

Jim smiled, swished the briny water with his hand, and said, "No, and you know my promise is good to support you in attending a great Presbyterian seminary like Columbia."

I laughed. "That is certainly beyond my kin, Jim, with..."

He interrupted: "I've heard your testimony," he said laughing, "God made it clear to me many years ago that you would become one of his servants.

"Well, in a way that's what I wanted to talk to you about..."

"I knew this was coming!"

"You remember the Adam mission-- kind of a ministry-- June and I believe God wants us to do."

"Of course, I've been praying for your vision of adopting men coming out of prison."

Though Jim had orchestrated my release from prison after visiting me in lockup several times, and it had been three years since my release, I was overwhelmed that a man of his stature had taken such a deep interest in me. I didn't know what to say and remained silent as I stepped into deeper water.

Jim rescued me: "Something must be troubling you."

"It's hard for me to tell you," I said as I turned to face him and the shore. "It's..it's about leaving the newspaper."

Jim stopped wading, and when he spoke his voice rose a half octave into a question: "What's that?"

A nervous grin tweaked the corners of my mouth. "I'm praying about leaving the Times-Union right away to go into full-time ministry."

"Whoa, boy; we do need to talk about that!" He moved away from me, gestured for me to follow him, returned to the beach and paced up and down like a hyped-up lifeguard about to deliver a safety-first speech to white-footed beachgoers facing the boisterous sea for the first time. Finally, he stopped, turned, pointed a long finger at me and said, "Now, I know why you're as troubled as the sea. That's a big step...a big leap into unknown waters."

I laughed. "You sound like I'm about to drown."

He laughed and held up palms to question me without a word.

The eight-year-old kid in me wasn't ready to answer him so I ran into the waves and chased a few of them down the beach.

Jim followed along, some distance behind me, but stayed on the shore. When I waded back into knee deep water, I wondered what he was thinking, but still didn't know what to say to him. I stood for a moment with my back turned to him on the shore, and felt my bare feet sinking into the cool sandy ocean bottom. Cooler-than-the-water ooze soothed my warm feet and bubbled between my toes, but as the undercurrent began to tug at my legs I felt uncomfortable. I coughed and yelled back to Jim, "I feel totally inadequate."

Jim stepped back into the ocean, sloshed up beside me, and in one motion scooped and splashed salty water on his chest and shoulders. "When I stood with you as your Best Man, as we watched June coming down the aisle, didn't you know God sent her to you to strengthen you for his purposes?"

234

Joy stirred my soul like the churning water and I said, "Thanks for saying that; what a tremendous blessing she is!"

Jim's face beamed. "I remember an early morning walk and talk on this very beach last year when I told you God put June in your life just as surely as he had placed Doris in mine."

Tears wet my eyes. Jim noticed, laughed and said, "He never changes his mind about his purpose for your life or his choice for your wife...they go hand-in-hand."

"Yes," I said, overwhelmed by the truth he had spoken and the picture of June walking hand-in-hand with me.

Jim nodded. "God has blessed you and me for sure with wives who stand behind us and with us, but this ministry thing is a matter of timing."

"Absolutely; June and I have prayed about it, and she's okay with my going full time soon...June and I... Dan and Sandra Jones met a couple of Sundays ago to talk about it." Jim moved closer to me and pointed to the waves crashing on the shore, turned and placed his hand on my shoulder. But his words focused on Dan Jones rather than on me: "Terrific man, great perspective, a leader on the Northside who cares about Jacksonville and its people."

"Exactly... we prayed about my organizing a new ministry... he said the first step was to get my pastor's blessing and then come to you for your approval."

A perplexed look darkened Jim's face. "Harold Hunter. Did you get Pastor Hunter's blessing?"

"Yes, he told me that if God was stirring me out of the nest at the newspaper like an eagle does with its young...my heavenly father would teach me how to fly."

Jim chuckled, ran his fingers through his white hair as if he was measuring it and said, "Sounds like Hunter; no wonder we have nicknamed him, Moses, a humble man of great faith, but that picture of you disturbs me."

To lighten his mood, I smiled, touched his shoulder, directed his attention to seagulls flying overhead and sang a line from a favorite prison hymn:"Like a bird from prison bars have flown, I'll fly away."

Jim laughed but didn't say anything, so I said, "God used you to set me free to serve him, but I want your approval to fly the coop."

I wasn't prepared for Jim's response.

38

He turned and held my eyes with his. Though only ten years my senior at sixty-two, the gentle look of a reluctant father about to correct a grown son crossed Jim's face, but then with force he declared, "Coop, you may not be ready to fly into full time ministry now! Go to seminary first. I'll help you the first year; besides three years out of prison is not a lot of time to get adjusted to the fast pace of life out here, much less build a foundation for a faith-based ministry."

My leader wasn't budging so I laughed, resorted to a dramatic metaphor, pointed at the ocean and said, "Moses didn't test the water before he plunged into the water to cross the Red Sea."

Jim forced a smile and said, "That's true, but you're not Moses and you don't have Pharaoh's army storming down on you from behind."

It tickled me that my stern-mannered mentor would top my play on word pictures to make his point, but I thought for a minute and fought back: "Only if drowning Pharaoh just happens to be God's calling for my life."

Jim was equally amused. He laughed but didn't back off. He said, "Ken, I'm glad you said that. Writing about Pharaoh's Waterloo instead of saving him could be your calling."

He topped me again! I knew exactly what he was saying, but replied, "That's too metaphorical for me; please put it in down to earth newsprint I can understand."

The quick-witted editor raised his head, gazed into the sky, pointed a long finger toward the seagulls that had soared to new heights above the earth, upward toward the puffy white clouds that ruled the sky. He motioned in their direction, raised his voice above the roar of the ocean breakers and blasted, "Before you fly away like those birds, let's go fly a *Ben Franklin kite.*"

Jim's theatrics and reference to his hero amused me even more and stimulated my imagination. I glanced up at the blue canapé covering us, half expecting to see a kite flying beneath a thunderhead ready to flash a bolt of lightning. Instead I saw the gathering of Laughing Gulls riding the air currents above us, descending to about a hundred feet, "laughing," circling as they looked for the next meal they could steal.

As Jim moved forward toward the seashore, I waded through the deep soft sand beneath my feet but managed to keep up with him. At water's edge, above the roar of the breakers, he stopped, flung his hands into the air and shouted in a high tenor voice that stirred up the sea gulls. They zoomed down to gawk and squawk at him, apparently thinking he held their next meal. Jim pointed at them and pronounced: "'Geese are but geese tho' we may think em swans; and Truth will be Truth tho' it sometimes proves mortifying and distasteful.'"

Not knowing what to say in response to Jim's Franklinism that spoke so powerfully to our debate, I smiled and repeated the familiar quote with a question in my voice:

'"Geese are but geese tho' we may think 'em swans; and Truth will be Truth tho' it sometimes proves mortifying and distasteful?"'

Jim laughed and said, "Quoted verbatim but don't you think that ole Ben is telling you the truth that even if it seems mortifying and distasteful to you, you shouldn't fly away from the newspaper business now."

Taken aback by his adamant stand and fervent language, I was silent so Jim turned toward me and shouted, "Is Ben not telling you the truth, Coop?"

"Probably!" I declared to give myself a chance to regroup. Then without the slightest idea of what I was going to say, I pointed at the birds overhead and said, "Seagulls are but seagulls, though we may think 'em...though we may think 'em... *Ea*-gulls."

Jim laughed and laughed, a weird kind of laughter, choked a bit, then demanded, "Say it again, man, say it again...that's brilliant!"

Confused that he was stoked by my response, I felt flabbergasted but nevertheless marched over to him like a soldier who had just defeated a mighty foe, placed my hand on his shoulder and with a raspy voice whispered in his ear, "Seagulls are but seagulls, though we may think 'em *Ea*-gulls."

"How in the world did you come up with that?"

"It came to me out of the blue."

"You lucky bird, you don't have the foggiest idea why even Franklin could have no comeback for that, do you?"

"No, I'm shocked?"

Jim took on the look of a college history professor and said, "Old Ben, the ultimate poet, if he were here, could not possibly top a poem in which you rhymed eagle with seagull when Franklin fought so hard to get the *turkey*, rather than the *eagle,* named the national bird for the land of the free."

I laughed and said, "I'm glad neither the turkey... nor the seagull won; the eagle is the perfect picture of freedom for America just as these seagulls are for me."

"I'm glad for you, and the truth of it will set you free to discover God's plan for you."

The depth of his remark stunned me, so I said something that sounded stupid as it came out of my mouth, "You mean, out here in the free world I can soar like a seagull though I may think I'm an eagle."

Jim guffawed and slapped the water, but finally managed to say, "Well, yes, in a manner of speaking; that's a little harsh though you may still see yourself as a bandit bird, Ken, but what I really mean is that the truth sets one free from fear, free from worry... to pursue the higher things in life, to make the right choices, to follow and fulfill one's destiny..."

I interrupted the newspaperman turned philosopher: "Wow! Ben Franklin couldn't have described freedom any better than that!"

Jim nodded his head in agreement, cleared his throat, tried to hide a tear in his eye, pointed toward the shore and said, "I've been a little too protective of you; you're right, kid. You're free! Go now; go now! Follow your star and fulfill your destiny."

Emotionally overwhelmed by my hero's magnificent heartfelt blessing, through tears I said, "Till this moment I never knew how important your blessing is."

A boyish look brightened the tall Irishman's countenance and he said, "I can do better than that, my man. I'll send you off with a quote more appropriate than one of Ben Franklin's ... a quote from a Gentleman Bank Robber turned minister."

For some reason his reference that I would become a minister whizzed past me, and I stood silent and still, watching my champion, waiting for another proclamation from Franklin.

To set the stage for his announcement and an inflated ceremony befitting the occasion, he waded toward me, slowly extended his long arms as if he were going to baptize me, placed warm hands on my shoulders, looked into my eyes, paused and declared, "Each day's doing; not yesterday's dark deeds defines one's destiny."

THE END

Afterword

A prisoner introduces "The Rest of the Story:"

(Many *years ago, Ken served a year in prison with a youth named TITO GONZALEZ and has remained close to him during his years in prison. A typewritten version of Tito's letter follows. Reading it one would think that he knew the title and theme of the book, but he didn't.*

12-18-13

Dear Ken & June,

Am thankful this holiday season for friends. Am thankful for both of you. I realize it's been a very difficult year for you but my heart and prayers have been with you. I learned as a young man that there are things in life more important than freedom. Doing what you were designed in life to do, living out your God ordained purpose—that's freedom. It, freedom, has nothing, absolutely nothing to do with a barbed-wire fence holding you in.

When I think of you two I see freedom in action. You've found what God called you to do. And you inspire me to live free. I never feel freer than when I sit behind a piano & usher in God's Presence. Being on the other side of this fence could never truly define freedom for me, For that, I thank you two. You've always encouraged me to pursue God. Thank you for your example, Papa Ken & Mama June! I love you both so much.

Your Timothy & Titus,

Tito

A former prisoner has the last word.

JULIE SEALS, a seventeen-year Meth addict, gave her life to Christ in a federal prison. Since her release thirteen years ago she has reconciled with her son whom she hadn't seen for seventeen years. A Christian young man, Tyler now prays for Julie who serves on the KCPM Evangelism Team with her husband, Mike, as a gifted speaker and singer. She wrote the following:

February 8, 2014

Dear "Papa Ken" Cooper:

Two years ago, when a retired banker named Hugh Jones, asked me, "Have you ever heard of Ken Cooper, the Gentleman Bank Robber?" – it was a question that changed my life!

My husband Mike and I were so excited the Saturday morning we piled into Hugh's car and drove out to the KCPM five acre ministry campus in North Jacksonville to meet you. I remember thinking how peaceful and serene it was with your quaint white country home at the front of your property and the sprinkling of other brick and stucco cottages and apartments over the lush, green landscape. As the four of us became acquainted and shared our testimonies, I realized I had never met a more sincere, humble man that you!

You introduced us to some of your Adam (Adopt A Man) men who resided in your transition houses, and I will never forget the joy on their faces or the way their eyes lit up as they told Mike and I all about how they rode a bicycle for the first time in over 30 years, went grocery shopping, cooked their own meals, and helped you care for the grounds. They were so profoundly grateful for the tiniest things that most of society takes for granted. And it was quite obvious how much the men deeply love you and "Mama June."

243

To my great delight, you gave us an autographed copy of your book, *Held Hostage*, that morning. I devoured that book in a matter of two days; I simply could not put it down! What a story! Ken Cooper, serial bank robber turned compassionate prison minister! Wow! You and June are now known for founding the hugely successful reentry housing prison ministries, Prisoners of Christ, Jacksonville, and the House of Hope, Gainesville, along with your tireless evangelism work that you both do in the Florida state prisons while still housing four long term ex-offenders on your five acre KCPM campus. Honestly, Mike and I were truly blown away that you gave us the privilege of stepping into prison ministry with you to ease your work load. What a blessing! An honor! What joy we have experienced traveling across Florida with you in *Abraham*, the beautiful 2010 Lincoln MKX that a Tampa family donated to Ken Cooper Ministries. Amazing grace.

During this time that Mike and I have accompanied you into prisons to preach the gospel and bring hope to incarcerated men and women, we have been deeply and permanently changed! It is impossible to properly convey the JOY and the HOPE that we see in the precious men and women in the prisons when you preach about the love, forgiveness, and life-transforming power of Jesus Christ. And now, you can add two more transformed people to that list!

With all our love in the Lord,

Julie Seals

Free!

$9.99 All proceeds benefit KCPM,
a 501(C)3 tax exempt prison ministry,
ten percent to Kairos Prison Ministry.

Order soft cover printed copies:

KCPM Publishing
P.O. Box 77160, Jacksonville, FL 32226

Order e-copies:

Visit: www.kencooperministries.org

For free copies *to prison libraries*

Contact Ken Cooper Prison Ministry
Email: coop3631@bellsouth.net

Be!

Close Encounters with Me

Look for Ken's third book,
coming soon, if the Lord tarries.
"Even so, come, Lord Jesus!"